AS FOR ME AND MY

CRAZY

HOUSE

LEARNING TO PROTECT YOUR HEART, MARRIAGE, AND FAMILY FROM THE DEMANDS OF YOUTH MINISTRY

BRIAN BERRY

As For Me and My [Crazy] House: Learning to Protect Your Heart, Marriage, and Family From the Demands of Youth Ministry

group.com
simplyyouthministry.com

Unless otherwise indicated, all Scripture quotations are taken from THE HOLY BIBLE, NEW INTERNATIONAL VERSION®, NIV® Copyright © 1973, 1978, 1984, 2011 by Biblica, Inc.™ Used by permission. All rights reserved worldwide.

Scripture quotations marked NASB are taken from the NEW AMERICAN STANDARD BIBLE®, Copyright © 1960,1962,1963,1968,1971,1972,1973,1975,1977,1995 by The Lockman Foundation. Used by permission.

Credits
Author: Brian Berry
Executive Developer: Nadim Najm
Chief Creative Officer: Joani Schultz
Editor: Rob Cunningham
Art Director: Veronica Lucas
Production Manager: DeAnne Lear

ISBN 978-0-7644-7553-5

10 9 8 7 6 5 4 3 2 1   20 19 18 17 16 15 14 13 12

Printed in the United States of America.

DEDICATION

To my wife and kids, who make all I do worth it. I love you.

CONTENTS

FOREWORD

I'm not a fan of balance.

Maybe I should rephrase that. Balance is fine, but I think we delude ourselves when we pretend it's achievable. I have often said that balance is something I only experience when I'm swinging past it on my pendulum swing from one extreme to its opposite.

I'll even take that hyperbolic statement further: I don't think balance is a biblical value. Balance is, as I see it, an American value. It's a rational idea, born out of our obsession with systematizing.

You might think I'm nuts or merely exposing my subconscious justifications for my own imbalance. And you might be right. But even if we approach the question of balance from a purely pragmatic perspective, it simply doesn't work. Matthew Kelly, in his helpful book, *Off Balance*, shows that decades of efforts in the business world to address the "work/life balance problem" hasn't increased workers' satisfaction—with either their work or personal life—even a smidge. In fact, as a whole, we are a *less satisfied* people than we were before all of these efforts.

There are better (and more biblical) ways of thinking and living. Sustainability comes to mind. The Old Testament approach to letting fields lie fallow every seven years isn't a picture of balance; it's a picture of sustainability. Jesus pulling aside by himself to pray wasn't an issue of his reaching a point of equilibrium; it was about the Son staying deeply connected to the Father, so his integrated, passionate, all-in life was sustainable and effective.

Life in youth ministry (or any church role, for that matter) isn't easily partitioned off into work buckets and home buckets. Our best lives are integrated. Sure, we need boundaries. Yes, we have to turn off our cell phones and intentionally disconnect from the never-ending demands of youth ministry. Absolutely, we need to prioritize our own spouses and children over the non-stop needs of others. But this best life isn't one of stasis. Our best life—the one that gives the most to the kingdom *and* provides the deepest satisfaction—isn't a teeter-totter in limbo.

I'm drafting this foreword on a Sunday morning, sitting in my backyard. My eighth-grade son is playing drums in the middle school worship band at this moment. My wife just woke up and is getting a cup of coffee. My high school senior daughter is still sleeping, but we'll soon head to church together. I'm "working" on a Sunday morning. That doesn't compute if my goal is balance. But in a scheme of sustainability, it makes perfect sense. Last night we had a fantastic family night, eating dinner together and watching *Home Alone*. By writing now, I can be more present to my family later in the day, when they desire my presence. Writing, this morning, isn't a choice of balance, but it sure is a choice of sustainability and satisfaction.

Brian Berry understands this. Brian is 100 percent all in. He gives himself completely to his wife and five children. He gives himself completely to the youth ministry at his church. He gives himself completely to his friends, to his parents, to his Savior.

I have the privilege of observing Brian's life close-up. He's the youth pastor at my church. My own daughter is a student leader in his high school ministry. Brian's freshman son, T.J., was in my middle school guys small group for three years. I'm currently the small group leader for Brian's second son, Tyler (who's in sixth grade). Brian was a participant in my coaching program for a year—a year in which he wrestled with many of the ideas in this book. And Brian is a close friend and confidant, often sitting in my backyard for hours of conversation about how we can be better youth workers, better husbands, better fathers, better Jesus-followers.

From this close-up perspective, I can state with certainty: Brian Berry's life is not a model for balance. The dude is way overcommitted. I worry about him, because he's one of the busiest guys I know.

But I can also state these facts with certainty:

1. Brian leads a stellar, world-class youth ministry.

2. Brian effectively empowers and serves a team of pastors who lead ministries from birth through young adults in our church.

3. Brian finds time for writing and speaking and teaching other youth workers.

4. Brian fluidly leads the youth workers network for our area.

5. Brian's wife gets lots of his attention and focus.

6. Brian's children all feel loved and known by their dad (his two sons that I know best revere him and aspire to be more like him—he is unequivocally their hero).

7. And Brian aces the seminary classes that usually bore and annoy him.

Brian Berry is the poster child of imbalance. But his integrated life is one of gorgeous sustainability. To be sure, his life is always teetering on the edge of unsustainability.

But maybe teetering on the edge of unsustainability, without tipping over, is the best, all-in, passionate life Jesus dreams of for us when he promises (in John 10:10), *"I have come that they may have life, and have it to the full."*

In this fantastic book you're about to read, Brian doesn't position himself as a model or an expert, but a fellow traveler. However, you could do a lot worse than to learn from the imbalanced-yet-sustainable, full life of this author, my friend.

Mark Oestreicher

Marko is a partner in The Youth Cartel, the author of many books for youth workers, teenagers, and parents, and a youth ministry volunteer at Journey Community Church.

INTRODUCTION

If this book had a birthplace, it would be June 2006 in Dana Point, California. My wife, Shannon, and I had gone away for two days of kid-free living to celebrate our 12-year anniversary. We do this trip annually, always around this time of year but not always at the same place. We'd been married for over a decade, and for whatever reason, I had spent a lot of time praying about this retreat and asking God to give us some specific direction. I'd never actually taken notes to a dinner date with my wife, but this time I did. I had written three thoughts I felt like God had led me to in the weeks leading up to our time together. I had come to three conclusions I wanted to run by my wife and to have us spend the next couple of days honestly asking, "How well are we doing with these?" Not like a formula or a workbook to fill out, but a conversation to be had.

As we sat down to dinner and after we had ordered our meal, I said, "I've been thinking and praying, and I think I've come to some conclusions I want to share with you. I'm hoping they encourage you and inspire us. I'm hoping they help us be who God has called us to be as individuals, as a couple, and as parents." Then I read off the three thoughts I'd written down:

1. The best gift we each can give our marriage is a healthy self.

2. The best gift we can give our family is a healthy marriage.

3. The best gift we can give our community and ministry is a healthy family.

I know there's nothing earth-shattering in those three statements. You probably read them and said, "Yeah, that sounds right." My wife didn't look at me and say I was talking crazy either. But we did agree that while these ideas sounded good, our house is CRAZY and living them out is not that easy. Sounding right and living right are radically different. The truth is, my experience and observation would show that I don't have a lot of Christian ministry lives, marriages, and families that I can point to and say, "Let's do what they do." Sure, I have a few. But seriously, only a few—and honestly, that is ridiculous.

As a community of followers of Jesus, we tend to collectively agree that God calls us to a relationship with God as our first priority. Then God calls some of us to marriage and perhaps to start a family. Finally, we would say that God calls us into a vocation. Even if our vocation call came first, the calling to marriage and family still trumps the vocation calling every time. Think about this choice: Quit your job or quit your family. Is that even a real question? If it is, you might need a different book than this one.

But while these values look all nice and pretty on paper or sound like a great three-point sermon outline, living them out is an entirely different thing. Keeping them a reality where the rubber meets the road is, in my experience, much more easily said than done. This book is an invitation to join me in that journey. So what you hold in your hands is not a project or a dissertation. I have no doctorate to justify or huge study to promote. I didn't spend a year literally trying to apply every Bible passage I could find on parenting or marriage to my home so I could write this book. I didn't interview thousands of Christian pastors, spouses, and parents to prove it. I just live it every day.

I'm a follower of Jesus. I'm a husband. I'm a dad to five children—three the old-fashioned way and two by adoption. I'm a pastor to a generation of kids and young adults in my local church. And I trust that as you read, you'll find that I'm a lot like you.

Hear me on this. This is not a book of stuff I've mastered. It's just the stuff I yearn for and am trying to embody. It's the stuff of real life. If you cut me, I bleed it. But like you, some days are better than others. Some days you shouldn't follow me around with a film crew. That would be bad. So as much as what you hold in your hands is the stuff of my soul, I pray that as you turn the pages, you find it to be the stuff of our collective soul. I hope it's the stuff that we all wrestle with as followers of Jesus, the stuff we strive for as spouses, and the stuff we yearn for as parents.

So if you keep reading, "Welcome to my world." Or maybe I should say, "Welcome to our world."

WHO AM I?

I'm not famous. This is not my first published work, but it is my first published book. I'm not sure exactly how you managed to get this book in your hands. Maybe you're my mom. (Hi, Mom!) Maybe you're a former student, or maybe you read my blog and therefore you know me a little. Maybe you've heard me teach somewhere or read a column I wrote somewhere in a magazine, or maybe you were bored and accidentally picked this book up. I dunno.

But just in case we don't go way back, let me tell you a little about the author of the book you are about to read. I hope this helps you understand and know me as we journey together through these pages. This is not just a book I wrote, but rather a life I'm trying to lead. It's about taking care of yourself, your marriage, and your family while doing life in ministry. Here's my brief story to date:

FIRST CAME LOVE: I was 13 when I committed my life to following Jesus after my girlfriend invited me to church. No, I'm not suggesting the "missionary dating" model or saying that high school dating is a great plan—in fact, far from it. But it is my story, and that girlfriend from high school eventually—after a long, seven-year dating stint—became my fiancée.

THEN CAME YOUTH MINISTRY: After serving and doing life in my youth ministry for four years as a high school student, I went off to the University of California at Davis. The summer after my freshman year, through a series of conversations and confirmations from God and mentors, I decided to do a summer internship in my old high school ministry. My plan was to serve God and students while working on a construction site for three months. I did do that, but what I received was far more than what I gave. I told my youth pastor, my high school sweetheart, my parents, and some trusted friends that I was not going to be an architect; God was calling me into youth ministry. I went back to Davis, changed my major, and tried to learn everything I thought I might use one day in ministry. I took a job driving buses. I learned Spanish for mission trips. I soaked up every teaching opportunity anyone would even remotely entrust me with. I kept doing internships, and eventually it led me to take a job as a camp speaker for another church's water ski trip the summer between my junior and senior years. That same summer, about a month earlier, I became engaged and turned the corner of my life toward college graduation and marriage. While teaching at that ski trip, I discovered the church was searching for a new youth pastor, and much to my surprise, the pastor search team asked me to turn in an application. I went back to school, sent the church my résumé and application, and figured out I could graduate a quarter early if I took a heavy load for two quarters. Several months later, I found out that I got the job. So I graduated in April, took a one-week vacation to the Grand Canyon with a friend, and then started my full-time job as a youth pastor, just weeks after my 22nd birthday.

THEN CAME MARRIAGE: I started my job as a youth pastor at the Evangelical Free Church of Fremont, California, in April 1994, and in June, I walked the aisle, and Shannon and I were married. That was nearly 18 years ago, and while not every day has been easy, we are still happily married, striving to stay in love and grow in our devotion to Jesus.

THEN CAME KIDS: Eventually my wife and I started having kids. We had three boys (T.J., Tyler, and Jake), each about two-and-a-half years apart, and along the way I continued to do youth ministry. After 11 years of teeth-cutting and ministry-learning in Fremont, God moved us south to San Diego to Journey Community Church, where I've been the youth pastor since 2005.

THEN CAME ADOPTION: This could be an entire book in itself, but I'll just cut to the chase. My wife and I loved our boys but had always said that after our third boy, we would be open to adopting a girl if God ever led us in that direction. Eventually, in the summer of 2008, God did just that, and while we were on a mission trip to Uganda, God made it clear that we were to adopt twins named Becky and Billy. So in January 2009 we went back to Uganda for another month and returned home in February, almost instantly doubling our family with the addition of 5-year-old twins to our home.

THEN CAME THIS BOOK: My ministry, my marriage, my family, and my own life dreams have led me to this place where I am today. The pages that follow flow from it.

SECTION ONE

THE BEST GIFT
I CAN GIVE MY
MARRIAGE IS A
HEALTHY SELF

I'm sorry; I can't do that because I planned to go for a run this afternoon.

I can't help with our kids that weekend because that's my annual two-day personal getaway weekend.

I can't make that meeting because it's Sunday afternoon naptime and I have a date with my hammock.

I can't do that today. I set this time aside to think and pray and read.

If those statements just roll off your tongue and don't sound the least bit selfish or unrealistic to you, then you can probably skip this section. Otherwise, they beg the question: "When, if ever, is it OK for you to say no to others (even to your spouse or kids) so you can say yes to you?" Does God ever call me to look out for me?

We all know the Apostle Paul's call: *Do nothing out of selfish ambition or vain conceit. Rather, in humility value others above yourselves, not looking to your own interests but each of you to the interests of the others (Philippians 2:3-4).* This is the banner cry of the Christian. We're each called to be like Jesus and to say no to selfish desires. We're called to love others like we want to be loved. We're called to be servant leaders. Right?

Sorta.

If you've ever flown on a commercial airplane, then you've heard the preflight spiel from a flight attendant. Or maybe you haven't heard it because, like me, you ignore the command to turn off electronic devices and continue playing some game or updating your Facebook® on your phone. Anyway, whether you've heard it before or not, here is part of the speech. The flight attendant will say something like:

> "In the event of a loss of cabin pressure, an oxygen mask will automatically drop from the ceiling. To start the flow of oxygen, pull the mask towards you. Place it firmly over your nose and mouth, secure the elastic band behind your head, and breathe normally. Although the bag does not inflate, oxygen is flowing to the mask. If you are traveling with a child or someone who requires assistance, secure your mask on first, and then assist the other person. Keep your mask on until a uniformed crew member advises you to remove it."

I know; my memory is impressive. (OK, fine—I used a search engine to get the wording.[1]) Anyway, when I actually do listen, it always catches me off guard that they tell me to help myself before helping my kids. I assume they make this statement for a few reasons. (1) It is counterintuitive. Most parents would default to the needs of their small child before themselves in an emergency. Really, who is going to ignore the needs of a panicked child waving their arms at an oxygen mask they can't reach and don't know what to do with? Helping them is parental instinct. (2) Their lawyers made them say it. Just kidding. OK maybe this is a legit reason. If so, then there's a third reason. (3) They tell you this because it will save your life and therefore increase the likelihood that you'll be able to save your child's life. Failure to do this could result in both of you dying. That's not good. In this case, looking out for others first could kill you.

If you've ever taken a class on how to save someone who is drowning, then you know that a person who is drowning is in a state of panic and isn't looking out for anyone else. This is bad. It means they will do anything to stay alive, including accidentally drowning the person trying to save them. That actually happens a lot. This is why lifeguards carry that red buoy to throw. It's not just for effect in Baywatch and cool lifeguard pictures. Lifeguards swim out, and once they get close enough, they throw it for the victim to grab—instead of the lifeguard's neck. They actually teach you that it would be better to knock a drowning person unconscious to save their life than to lose yours in the process. Essentially we train lifeguards to look out for their own interest before the interest of others—and in this case, it is wise.

I wonder if the same is true of more than just airplane cabin pressure or someone drowning. Are there other times when the smartest thing we can do is to look out for our own well-being first?

The other day, I was reading this famous passage of Scripture. Our whole church was going through this statement Jesus made and dismantling it for weeks on end. People were challenged to memorize it. Small groups were studying it. Large group teachers were repeating it. We aren't much of a liturgy church, but during this weekend series, we all repeated it verbatim each week. In fact, this statement is so famous and so central that I, like I'm sure many of you, had it memorized before the series even began. But as Scripture has a way of doing, all that repetition made this statement from Jesus come alive to me in some crazy new ways. One day as I repeated it, this one phrase just jumped out at me.

You know the statement. Modern-day theologian and author Scot McKnight calls it "The Jesus Creed." It is this: " *'Hear, O Israel: The Lord our God, the Lord is one. Love the Lord your God with all your heart and with all your soul and with all your mind and with all your strength.' The second [commandment] is this: 'Love your neighbor as yourself.' There is no commandment greater than these"* (Mark 12:29-31). But the little phrase that jumped out at me comes near the very end—the two words *as yourself.* I'd never thought about it much, but as I did, I almost thought it was wrong. Maybe Jesus blew it or maybe Mark recorded it wrong. Jesus ended by saying we should love others like we love ourselves? Really? Perhaps it should say, "Love others like you want to be loved." Or maybe it should say, "Love others selflessly like those who truly love you." Or surely it should read, "Love others as God has loved you." But none of those are the model Jesus chose to use in this summary of God's commands. He didn't even use himself in this instance and say, "Love others as I have loved you." Instead he said to love others like you love yourself.

So let me ask you. If you loved others liked you love yourself, how loving would you be? What if you loved your spouse like you loved yourself? Would it mean you constantly demand that they ignore their own soul to meet your needs? Would it mean you never let them say no? If you loved your spouse like you loved yourself, would you constantly criticize them for not doing enough? Would it be a healthy love or a masochistic one?

If you're like me, you'll say no to the time you set aside for a run to meet with a student. You'll ditch a personal day to help your spouse or kids. You'll put yourself on the back burner regularly, and in an effort to help others, you'll stop helping you. It'll seem like a God-honoring choice.

But maybe, just maybe the best gift I can give anyone is a healthy me. Maybe, just maybe, the best thing you could do to love anyone else would be to start loving yourself.

CHAPTER ONE

AHHHHHH!...BEFORE YOU EXPLODE

IF you have started kicking puppies, cussing at students to get them to shut up, and giving your family the silent treatment at home, it might be time to focus on you.

As a kid I remember this one time when I was frustrated at life. I went to the back of the house and started beating a tennis ball against a wall, taking my angst out against this inanimate object because my mom said she and my sister were off limits, and my dad was at work. In college I once was so frustrated that I decided to go for a run to pound the angst out of my body, or at least get so tired that I had no energy for it anymore.

Then I became a pastor and got married and eventually started having a family, and the spaces to safely vent my frustrations diminished daily. I can't yell in the office. I can't kick a soccer ball against the sanctuary doors. I can't say what's really on my mind to the angry parent in front of me—or if I do, it will only make matters worse. I can get angry at home, but then I become the angry parent my kids hate or the irate husband my wife avoids.

It's not like I'm some kind of constantly angry explosion waiting for a place to ignite. It's just that life and ministry aren't always great, and most pastors that I know have a tendency to stuff that emotion down deep. Maybe, in part, that's because the ones who don't hide those emotions are just angry pastors no one wants to be around. If I'm honest, I stuff it a lot. But when there's no release, there's nothing for it to do but build until it eventually explodes—usually on the wrong person who was in the wrong place at the wrong time, and usually someone I love.

I once heard Billy Graham's wife, Ruth, say about her husband, "It's not my job to fix him. That's God's job. My job is to love him." I don't remember if I read it or heard it in an interview, but I remember that it impacted me. Here was a woman who clearly and confidently knew where she fit in the bigger picture of God's plan. She understood her role in her marriage, and she knew what was her problem and what was not. If she couldn't love Billy, that was her issue. If she couldn't fix Billy, that was an issue between Billy and God. I think that's profoundly true for each of us. It's not the job of our spouse or family or friend to tend our soul when it gets out of whack, and I can't blame anyone else for the funk either. It's my job, and I need to deal with it.

When I was in college, I had a roommate who was looking for a car. It was long before the days of Craigslist®; people still sold stuff the old-fashioned way. You made a flier with a picture or description of what you wanted to sell on the top of the page, and then put your contact info like 10 times across the bottom in little pre-cut tear-off strips so people who were interested could contact you. On my way out of class I saw one of those fliers with a picture of a creatively decorated 1972 Toyota® Corolla station wagon with about 400,000 miles on it. "Gretchen" was for sale for $500. The ad said she was a bit ugly but mechanically solid. I tore off the strip.

Later that night, I went with my roommate to go look at the car, and the man selling Gretchen promised that the car was reliable. "Put oil and water in her and keep her belts strong and she'll drive forever." He had records of virtually everything he'd repaired mechanically on the car for like a decade. I told my roommate that the man was probably right. I told him that if he checked the oil and water every time he added gas, he'd still have to fix some stuff now and then, but the car would likely drive just fine for at least another 100,000 miles. Toyota was famous for that kind of dependability.

Gretchen was ugly, and cosmetically she was a mess—filled with torn interior and painted by hand with green spray-paint—but she was worth $500. Again I warned my roommate, "You can't just add gas and go." He said, "OK. Got it."—and then proceeded to ask me if he could borrow $500 to buy the car. I agreed and gave him the money, and he soon started repaying me.

About $300 into the payments, his girlfriend's parents got a divorce, and she was told to come and get her stuff or never see it again. So he took Gretchen and his girlfriend down Interstate 5 on a steady 300-mile drive to Los Angeles, and the engine proved strong. Gretchen drove faithfully there and even made it halfway back before she just froze up. Seized solid. My roommate had driven all the way to L.A. and halfway back without ever checking the water or the oil. Gretchen died. Because she was filled with personal belongings, he paid to have her towed the rest of the way back to school, which cost him almost as much as the car did. Then he made the rest of the payments to me on a dead car he no longer could drive.

Sometimes, I think we treat ourselves like my Chris treated Gretchen. (Oops! Sorry, Chris. I meant to keep you anonymous, but it slipped. My bad. Good thing you married Michele. Guess that makes it worth it.) Anyway, I think that deep down, we believe we'll be fine. We've seen the warning signs. The gauges on the dashboard are warning us there's a problem. But we keep going. We've been here before; we'll get through it again.

Then, after failing to take care of our soul for so long, never venting our anger, never loving ourselves, and never dealing with our junk, things heat up, our soul just freezes, and it's game over. I've heard some proudly say, "I'd rather burn out than rust out." Problem is, either way you're out.

CHAPTER TWO

CAN I BE REAL WITH YOU?

WHEN our boys were little, they found great joy in naked running. No, we didn't raise them in a nudist colony, but that didn't stop them from running naked wherever they could. Change a diaper without a new one ready to go, and they'd likely break free running naked. Give them a bath, get mostly dry, and sprinting naked would often ensue. They evidently found great joy and laughter in the hilarity of naked feet slapping the floor and unrestricted movement of clothing-free moments. We often would joke and call out "NAKED PARADE" as they went by laughing. We even have a child who, if you sent him to the bathroom, would strip naked to poop. We called him the Naked Pooper. Thankfully, he only did this at home.

But our kids are past the naked parade stage at this point and have grown up to have a sense of modesty about them (unless it's a bare butt, and then that's still hilarious—but that's another story). While I'm not advocating a nudist world and most people don't want to see you or me naked, there is something sad about my kids' lost innocence. There's also a deeper truth that as we grow up, the spaces where we can just be our "naked" selves, without having to impress people or even prove ourselves, diminish rapidly.

As a pastor, I can't share my struggles with everyone because it's draining. At times, I can't share it simply because I don't want it as part of my workplace. It's not that I don't want to be open; it's just that I don't want to talk about it while planning the weekend retreat. Maybe that makes sense to you. Maybe not. But either way, safe places where I can be the fully vulnerable me are few and far between these days.

As a youth pastor, I can't share most of my struggles because it's inappropriate for my audience. Even when I say to students in a small group, "Come as you are and share your life openly," I can't fully reciprocate. It's just not appropriate for much of my life to be accessible and accountable to a 14-year-old student. So I share openly the good and bad but not the whole story.

I know you're supposed to share everything with your spouse, but the honest truth is that I think some of my job as a pastor isn't stuff my wife needs to worry about either. Some of it is confidential. Some of it just wouldn't benefit her own faith or our marriage if she knew all the details. I don't need my dinner table turning into an elder board meeting. I could go on, but here's the bottom line: It's hard to find safe people to be open with. It's so hard that it's just more common for pastors and people in ministry to share with no one instead of someone.

If you're like me, then you've tried to defeat this reality but you've been burned. You've opened your life, and the searing comments of a wounded confidant have been too hard to overcome. You shared your life with a friend and found the prayer requests of another to have opened your life like a book to be read by all. So this chapter has teeth to it. Living in a fish bowl can be its own kind of death.

But you and I have to defeat it. In an effort to be a healthy me, I cannot ignore my desperate need to be the real me. I need friends and mentors who can speak truth into my life. Proverbs 26:12 tells us this: *Do you see a person wise in their own eyes? There is more hope for a fool than for them.* I don't want to be a fool, and only fools think they can see all things clearly in the mirror. So I have sought out friends, mostly fellow pastors in my community who are now dear friends. We often get together casually all year and then annually in a four-day stint to dig really deep. We snag a retreat spot and eat and pray and think and dig into one another's lives for four days.

That idea was part of what Shannon and I concluded on our retreat to Dana Point I told you about earlier, and it's proved invaluable to the pursuit of a healthy me. These men and a select few others are the ones to whom I truly open my whole life. They're the ones with whom I can talk about work, about marriage, about hope, about dreams, about fears, and about life. They're the ones I call when it's not going right. They're the ones I reach out to and share joys when I know they will celebrate with me without a hint of jealousy over the great thing that has come my way. They are the ones who help me stay sane. They help me be the me that God called me to be. They help me bring the best me to the space of my marriage, my family, and my ministry. I owe them a lot.

Who isn't impressed by you? Who are the people who are not looking to you for guidance and who don't need you to be anything but you? Who can speak the real truth to you, and who has the keys to open any door God leads them to? Who are the people who are not invested in your ministry and have no axe to grind or ground to defend? Who are the ones that you can be the naked you before?

CHAPTER THREE

MENTOR ME, OBI-WAN KENOBI

LUKE had Obi-Wan Kenobi and Yoda. Robin had Batman. The Karate Kid had Mr. Miyagi. Timothy had Paul. Peter had Jesus. I had my dad, my youth pastor, and Moses.

OK, we called him Moses; his real name is Ron. But seriously, he was Moses in the flesh. Every Tuesday night for a year, I met friends in a grocery store parking lot and we carpooled across the San Francisco Bay to Palo Alto. Forty-five minutes later, we'd pull up in front of his house, and by the time we got out of the car and turned our eyes to the steps, there on the porch would be Moses: a tall, barefoot, bearded man wearing white, with a gold alpha and omega pendant that hung on a gold chain and settled in his silver chest hair, peeking out of the top of his shirt. How could anyone ever forget this kind of detail?

His arms open wide and his smile large, he'd welcome each of us to his house with an embrace and then invite us in for fresh fruit, cheese, crackers, fellowship, and the simplicity of studying the Word. Ron is the most gentle and unassuming man you'll ever meet. He just genuinely loves God, wants to raise up disciples of Jesus, and seeks to be faithful to the Word of God. To that end, eight or nine men from all walks of life showed up on this 70-year-old pastor's porch for the "Timothy Discipleship Program" to study Ephesians and then have dinner under his tutelage. It was a year of meals, mentoring, and ministry together. It was life-changing.

Ron was the first man to correct me in prayer. Seriously, he told me I used God's name like it was a comma. He challenged me to talk to God like God was a real person, not in the prayer patterns I'd been taught by men. He also taught me what I affectionately now embrace as the "toast prayer." We'd walk into the same Italian restaurant, and he'd hug the waitress in a way only Moses could do with his humble and genuine Jesus-like charisma. We'd then grab our "usual table" and order our meal. Meals changed from time to time, but drinks often did not. Ron always got a glass of white Mondavi® wine, and before the meal, he'd ask one of us to pray.

By "pray," Moses did not mean close your eyes and talk in a special voice or with special words to a deity. He meant, "Raise your glass, and like a lover of Jesus, gladly thank him for the friends around the table, the conversation, and the food as you invite his Holy Spirit to just spill all over the table." No one bowed their heads, and therefore no one quietly wondered if we'd be interrupted by our waitress bringing orders. We just toasted God in prayer. It was like breathing fresh crisp mountain air for the first time in a long time. It filled my soul and felt totally right. Go to dinner with me sometime. I'll teach you my mentor's ways.

Moses'—um, Ron's—leading shaped my story. My wife and I made the sacrifice of time in our family. I asked to get out of a year of monthly Tuesday night church pastor/elder meetings so I could invest in my soul. I never had a grandfather that took me to church or talked to me about faith, formation, or manhood. This was my chance. I seized it and soaked it up.

Paul told Timothy that it was his call to pour into others in the same way that Paul poured into him. *And the things you have heard me say in the presence of many witnesses entrust to reliable people who will also be qualified to teach others (2 Timothy 2:2).* Jesus told his disciples to do the same with the investment he made in them by making disciples. *"All authority in heaven and on earth has been given to me. Therefore go and make disciples of all nations, baptizing them in the name of the Father and of the Son and of the Holy Spirit, and teaching them to obey everything I have commanded you. And surely I am with you always, to the very end of the age" (Matthew 28:18-20).* None of this is news to anyone reading this book.

There's just one problem, however. The need for a mentor in the lives of the disciples did not stop when Jesus was resurrected any more than Timothy's discipleship was done when Paul died. We must continue to not only raise up disciples, but also be discipled ourselves. Yes, the Holy Spirit and God's Word play an important role in this process. But every seasoned Christian knows that there is wisdom in the experience of an older mentor that simply cannot be ignored without being a fool.

I have often told students in my ministry that there are only two ways to learn things. One is the hard way and the other is from someone who learned it the hard way. The first is the tough, windy road through the school of hard knocks. The second is a quiet, rarely traveled trail that is filled with wisdom and the discernment of a proven guide who has been there, done that, and has the wounds to show it. If I want to be the best me God created me to be, I need mentors who will disciple me through the less-traveled path. When we choose the narrow trail, we choose the road that leads to a better marriage, fewer mistakes, and fewer arrogant regrets. The wise among us seek the wisdom of those around them.

Don't be a fool. Find a mentor.

CHAPTER FOUR

THE THING THAT AFFECTS EVERYTHING

I once heard someone say that the greatest sin of teenagers is not sexual addiction, anger, rebellion, gossip or even lust. They said it was "wasting time." Think about it. When you ask the average teenager in America what they did last summer, what do they say? My experience says that unless they came from a rich, world-touring family, they'll tell you they sat around doing nothing. Ask them what they did last weekend and you'll likely find it was so insignificant that they forgot. It's not that they are ignorant of the needs around them; it's just that a huge percentage of them are apathetic to them.

I wonder if the same is true of a lot of leaders when it comes to the truth about saying yes and no. We know that these words are powerful and set our lives on a specific course. We are not ignorant of this; we are just apathetic to it. We all know that a failure to manage these two tiny words in our lives can destroy us. We know they lead us into a lifetime of missed opportunities and doing stuff God never called us to do. We also know the power of a God-honoring yes or no. But despite this understanding, our actions would often say that we are evidently apathetic to this reality. It affects everything.

Maybe it's because most leaders I know are doers. They are "git-er-done" people. When they see a problem, they solve it. Good leaders embody the vision, inspire others to join them, and make great sacrifices to see it realized. Put another way, they are "yes people." If you're trying to get a project completed, it's not uncommon to find busy people and ask them to help you. You know who they are; they're the ones you always see doing stuff. They do this because they say yes.

This is the normal mode of operations for them, and as a leader, I love git-er-done people. I love yes people. I need yes people. I even want to be a git-er-done person. But the older I get, I also know I must be a "no person," too, or I can't be the "yes person" to the right things. The truth is, I say yes to stuff I should say no to and no to stuff I wish I could have said yes to because I said yes to that other thing too soon. I've had to work hard to wean myself of this tendency. I intrinsically recognize this struggle, but my ability or inability to manage it radically affects my ability to be present in my marriage, my family, and my ministry.

As a youth pastor, I must tend to an endless list of needs. No to-do list is ever fully done. Never have I been at the place where there was nothing to do or where all the needs of every program, let alone every individual student, were fully met. Never have I not needed more help or told my church, "No, send those resources elsewhere; we're set." Unless you're in a church that has 15 positions on your youth ministry payroll, you also likely have to be a jack–of-all-trades. You are responsible for finding or being the graphic artist, the travel agent, the administrator, the teacher, the shepherd, the janitor, and the manager. If you delegate it to another, then it's yours again when they are sick. I trust you're also a youth pastor by calling and therefore, like being a spouse or a parent, you cannot just shelve it when it's inconvenient. Most youth pastors that I know kind of fantasize about it: Wouldn't it be awesome, for a season, to work a 9-to-5 job or any job where you close the door and walk away? I'm jealous sometimes of students who have "nothing to do this weekend." Clock-in and clock-out sounds so amazing some days—and so far from my reality.

Probably the first time I consciously noticed this tendency in me to do too much in ministry was when my oldest son was born. Up to that point, both my wife and I were working full-time jobs. I was young, energetic, full of vision, and set on building a youth ministry that I could be proud of. I stayed up late, got up early for prayer meetings, and said yes to all kinds of stuff. We had youth ministry events all the time. Our life was full. As I watched my wife begin to nest and as I began to prepare my life for fatherhood, I knew I was on a path to failure if I didn't make some changes.

It reminded me of Moses—not Ron this time, but the real, biblical Moses. In Exodus 18, Moses had a problem. There were lots of people with disputes in the nation of Israel, and they needed him to be their judge and reveal God's will for each situation. Seeing the massive crowd gathered around him and the me-centered system that Moses had created, his father-in-law Jethro confronted him by saying, *"What you are doing is not good. You and these people who come to you will only wear yourselves out. The work is too heavy for you; you cannot handle it alone" (Exodus 18:17–18).*

I call it being "Jethroed." It's when you're doing something that seems right to you, but then some wise mentor looks at it and says, "You're crazy. Stop right now and rethink this." I felt as though God looked me right square in the face and said, "If you keep this up, you're going to wear out yourself and all those around you."

Has God ever said that to you? Has someone else ever told you that? No, not someone who is lazy and just wants you to slow down so they feel better about their inactivity. I mean someone who believes in you and the mission but knows that your life choices are leaving both of those in jeopardy. If so, then maybe it's time to heed the call. Maybe it's time to rethink your thinking and realize that you've mismanaged these two tiny words. Maybe, just maybe, what's standing between you and a healthy marriage, a healthy family, and a healthy ministry is entrenched in these words: Yes and No. Maybe it affects everything more than we want to admit.

"That's nice Brian, but you don't understand. I can't say no right now. My life is crazy and I can't cut anything."

OK, it's about to get a little crazy in here. I didn't make up the title for this book; I am the title of this book! I have five kids in three schools. As I type this, I have literally hundreds of other things I could be doing. I'm currently coaching two soccer teams and playing on one. I'm going to seminary one night a week for the sixth year in a row (don't ask for more details; it'll just result in an entire chapter of words). Because I teach during church on Sundays in our high school program, my family goes to our church's Friday night service. Our small groups meet on Wednesday night, and due to all of this, I have zero weeknights not committed to coaching soccer, church, or my seminary from mid-August through Thanksgiving. All five kids are playing soccer, so we have five games in three cities every Saturday.

Truth is, I need this chapter as much as you do. Maybe more so. Maybe your life story would make my to-do list or the demands on my life look like a trip to Disneyland®. If you're a single parent, I'm positive that's true. If you're a single parent with a full-time job and you're the volunteer youth pastor, too—game over. You win.

I don't claim to have some kind of "busy person trump card," and this isn't a pity party either. None of us needs to receive judgment or sympathy, or to become the poster child for the busy people of the world convention. Bottom line, we are just people reminding one another that we have to say yes and no intentionally and seriously. Surely Moses would have "gotten it."

I know I "get it"—and despite the long list of stuff I'm doing that I just confessed to you, I have had to say no to a lot to keep my life even remotely crazy and not totally insane. I have to say no to my kids' requests to play two sports during the same season. Out of principle, I say no to every request to do a retreat, event, serving day, or ministry meeting on Saturdays for that crazy 25 percent of the year. I vow to not schedule conflicts and to only miss two (or at most three) of the games of which I'm a coach all season.

I have to say no to the desire in me to just finish seminary because it would result in more time out and would increase the absentee dad factor to levels that are unacceptable to me. I have stuff that needs fixing around my house and projects left incomplete and things I'd rather be doing. I have to say no to church meetings when my family needs me instead. I have to say no to my wife and kids and family and work and pretty much everyone to even find anything remotely close to "me time" to tend to my soul or body or mind. It's ridiculously hard. It requires self-discipline, God's leading, and wisdom beyond my extended experience to sort through it all. Truth is, you and I cannot ignore this or blow it off as a nice idea either. We must stop saying yes to things we should say no to.

I recognize that we cannot and should not say no to everything. But I'm convinced that God is calling and equipping each of us. It is our job to respond to God's call and to learn to sort through the sea of demands, voices, and needs that mimic God's call so that we can do all that God truly has called us to and none of what God has not.

I must do this. You must do this. Our marriages, families, and ministries might not know it, but they all need us to do this as well.

CHAPTER FIVE

IT'S A BIRD, IT'S A PLANE, IT'S JESUS

I often listen to a radio morning show on my 15-minute drive to work. I enjoy it because the hosts are funny and always tell about some weird news piece or video they have linked to their website—and I dream up some way to use it for a slot in our weekend service. The other day they were riffing off some news article about vacation spots you should go to that no one else has heard of. It was really interesting as people called in and said, "You just have to go to such-and-such a place. It's amazing." One caller said something about a town that I wanted to go look up.

So I went looking for the show's website for the news report link and was surprised—not because of what I found out about the town, but because I had the wrong mental picture for all the voices of the radio show. The website has photos of the entire team and I found out that AJ was older than I thought while this guy named Hula is Polynesian. That makes sense now with a name like Hula, but I never would have guessed. A gal named Delana looks younger than I expected, and Dorothy was not at all like someone you'd see in the Wizard of Oz. The truth is, I had races, age, dress style, and hair color all wrong. For a second, I even wondered if this is really true. Surely this can't be "my" radio crew.

Maybe this is sacrilegious, but I think that might be what it will be like when Jesus returns. I really don't know, but my guess is that it will forever ruin the image of the skinny, longhaired, white man so many have embraced on religious posters and shrines. Maybe he'll be the wrong height, the wrong skin color, his robe will be the wrong shape, or the angels around him will have too many wings. My guess is that for many, it won't even be like running into someone you haven't seen in 40 years: "Jesus, is that really you?" Instead it will be more like, "Um, I'm sorry, but have we met before? How do you know my name?" I also think this confusion will at least partly be our fault. Let me explain.

I know it's not our intention, but maybe pastors enhance this distortion of what Jesus looked like. Maybe it's not because someone saw a picture of Jesus and got it wrong in a church hallway or on a really big Bible. Maybe it's because we've essentially told people that Jesus should look like us. It's not uncommon for us to tell people to be the hands and feet of Jesus. I'm guessing you've heard or even said to someone, "You could be the only Jesus they will see today. So ask God to give you his eyes and ears." I say this to inspire others to be, as Paul calls us, the body of Christ. *Now you are the body of Christ, and each one of you is a part of it (1 Corinthians 12:27). So it* seems noble. It seems right and good and in part, it is.

But here's where stuff gets crazy. There's a fine line between "you might be the only Jesus someone will see today" and "you are Jesus today." The former is about behaving like and being used by Jesus; the latter is thinking Jesus is dead and I need to be his replacement. As pastors, I think it's incredibly tempting to shift our gospel from Jesus-centered to me-centered. It's all too easy to stop pointing students *to* Jesus and to start being Jesus *for* students.

My lead pastor, Ed Noble, once said during a parenting summit we hosted that we have to make sure we don't "lead our kids to a Jesus we're going to have to unlead them to later." In other words, don't lead them to an unbiblical Jesus. As youth workers, this happens if we're leading people to ourselves. It's subtle, but before you know it, we have the royal robe on and people are starting to lose sight of the real Jesus and coming to us before they go to him. *Whoever claims to live in him must live as Jesus did (1 John 2:6).* "Live as Jesus" cannot be substituted for "Be Jesus." I know this truth, but some days I think I fall into the trap anyway.

When I was a youth pastor in Northern California, we did a collaborative prayer and worship event for a bunch of churches, and we were trying to inspire students to share their faith.

We wanted to use a candle illustration and have students pass the faith on. Then one of the pastors in our group spoke up and said this was a bad idea. I figured it was a fire code violation or something, but his objection was theological, not methodological. He said that we were subconsciously telling students that they were Jesus. If we wanted to do this exercise, we should still light the center candle. However, students should not pass the fire from candle to candle to the person next to them, he said. Instead, someone with a lit candle should go find someone with an unlit candle and then lead that person back to the center candle to get the light from the source. That way, instead of passing on the light of Jesus, students would be leading people back to Jesus himself.

We ended up deciding that, in fact, it would be a fire hazard if students walked all around inside a church with drippy, lit candles. Instead we did the same thing but without the actual fire, using glow sticks in buckets in the front of the room. Two students came and each got one, then found a friend who didn't have one and led them to the "Jesus buckets" to get one for themselves. My friend was right. We are not called to be Jesus; we are called to be *like* Jesus so that we can lead people to Jesus. There is a huge difference.

I want to be useful. I want to help students find Jesus. I want to be used by God for this purpose. But everyone, especially me, knows I am not God. I'm also not God's only available resource. God's kingdom will not fall apart when I die. Jesus does not look like me or only use me. He has a long list of people to use.

Throughout history, God has always had a way of accomplishing his will, with or without our willing involvement. Reminding myself of this fact is the only way I can even sleep some nights. I have to cast all my anxiety on God. I have to remind myself that this is not my deal and that I can quit trying to be "Super Jesus" with a modern-day cape.

Several years ago, I had taken a group of students to the beach, and one girl from our youth group also happened to be there on her own at the same time. I could see her but she couldn't see me. I got her mobile number from her friend and texted her some random note that was fun but a tiny bit creeper with details about her towel color and stuff. Because my number was not in her phone, she asked who I was. I told her I was Jesus. She didn't believe me and asked again. I repeated that I was Jesus and that this was how I knew so much about her.

Eventually I told her that she should join our group on another part of the beach while continuing to tell her other crazy facts about herself. It was all funny and silly, and eventually she found us and figured out it was me the whole time. As we joked, I told her she now had my cell phone number and that she should save it under the name "Jesus." So she did. For years, whenever I would call her, her phone would ring and her screen would tell her that "Jesus" was calling. We were just clowning around, but subtly, as a pastor it's easy for me to slip into that metaphor and turn a joke into an attempt at reality. I am not Jesus.

Maybe you and I should stop trying to be Jesus and just settle for being like him instead.

Trying to be Jesus is not a path to a healthy me. It is a path to a stressed-out me as I attempt to be something and someone I cannot possibly be. The best thing I can do for me and for everyone around me is to stop trying to be Jesus to anyone. Instead, I need to simply lead them back to the Jesus I know.

CHAPTER SIX

NO REST FOR
THE WEARY

"NO rest for the weary." Whoever said that was an idiot. Come to think of it, he might have actually been the uncle of one of the guys I used to ride mountain bikes with. Or maybe it was a pastor. Keep reading.

When I first moved to San Diego, the sunny weather had me rushing to be active outdoors. I tried surfing, kayaking, running, soccer, and hiking. I also tried biking, after hearing that a new friend of mine liked to mountain bike. Sounded fun and like something I'd like to try again. So one day I said, "I'd be game sometime and would love to ride with your crew one day if you're up for it." He said sure and invited me to come. It had been awhile since I had biked, but I grabbed my gear and headed out to meet these two guys at the trailhead. They always went at either 3 in the afternoon or around 6 a.m.—both were hard times for me to make work with my life and family—but I didn't know any routes to do on my own, so I was at the mercy of their schedule.

My bike was quite a bit older and less tricked-out than theirs, and these two guys were both older but in better biking shape than I was. As a result, they would lead me up and around all kinds of local dirt trails. I'd eventually fall behind and find them again, only waiting when there was a fork in the road they thought I might miss. They would wait and catch their breath at the top of some hill where the trail split, and when I'd see them, I'd think, "Phew, I need a break to catch my breath, too." Then as soon as I caught up to them, this one guy would say, "The last man gets the best workout; we're going this way. No rest for the weary." And then they'd take off. The result was that I was clearly holding them back, and I started to hate riding with them, eventually just stopping altogether.

I wanted to work out with friends. I also wanted to experience the joy of an accomplishment and rest together. The two were evidently incongruent.

Despite Jesus' words, ministry can often feel like this. I know Jesus said, *"Come to me, all you who are weary and burdened, and I will give you rest" (Matthew 11:28).* But rest? Really? Think about it. When was the last time you ran into a youth pastor at some local or national conference gathering and said, "Wow, it's great to see you. Really, how are you doing? How's ministry treating you these days?" and they answered, "Wow,

I'm great and really rested. I love ministry, it's such a peaceful calling. I can't imagine doing anything else." I've never once said that, and if I heard someone say that to me, I would either expect that they were living in a Tibetan monastery, practicing the fine art of sarcasm, or just straight-up lying.

Why is that? If Jesus is right, then pastors should lead the way in anxiety-free faith and restful trust that God is in control. All leaders will get weary, but surely pastors should be the quickest to give their burdens to the Jesus who wants to carry them, right? Evidently the answer is no? Maybe it's because of stuff we've already talked about in earlier chapters. Maybe it's because we don't say no very well. Maybe it's because we wear our Jesus hat backward and are trying to do his job for him. Or perhaps it's because we don't value rest over excellence. We don't value a soul at rest over ministry productivity. We clearly don't live in a culture that honors it, and it's hard to create an ethos in our churches, homes, or even personal lives that is much different.

In May 2000, I had a chance to go to Israel with my dad, my youth pastor, a close friend, and some mentors of mine; I jumped at the opportunity. I was so excited to go and see the history and walk where Jesus walked. As a result of all that we saw and learned while there, the trip impacted me deeply. But one of the most profound learnings for me didn't even occur in Israel. It happened on the way there, in the city of Milan, in northern Italy. We were switching planes and had an eight-hour layover there. Instead of just sitting in the airport, the trip organizers had booked a bus ride for us to some quaint town on the Italian side of the Swiss Alps to kill some time. So we drove into this beautiful lakeside community with the backdrop of the Alps behind it. When we arrived I immediately headed for some true espresso, ate some legit tiramisu, snapped some pics, and began poking around in little gift stores. But as I did, I started to consistently run into closed signs. I couldn't figure it out because it was like 3 p.m. This was literally foreign to me.

As I wandered around, I started to discover that it was because we were in a culture that valued a good nap. Seriously, the entire community shut down from like 3 to 5 p.m. for naptime. People even fell asleep on park benches, in cars, in lawns, all over the place. It was like someone flipped a switch and the entire community shut down—and then opened up again from like 5 to 8 p.m. I was so surprised. I was so jealous. It was like kindergarten, and I wanted to roll out my mat and join in. I remember sitting down in a park and being mesmerized and empowered by this lull in our trip.

I don't live in a culture that is anything like that, and it's hard to create an alternate one, too. In America we live in a culture that has phrases like, "I need a vacation from my vacation." Are you guilty of this? I am. I've "taken time off" and then had no time to breathe because my time off was just too packed with time exploring and doing. I love a good nap in my hammock while camping, but while that would seem like an easy thing to grab, the drive to do something with the kids or see something we have not seen yet often moves me out of rest and into motion.

At home, even the unplanned day off is hard to hold sacred—especially if the whole family is around. I recently talked to my oldest son about this and had to confess to him that I think I might be modeling a solid work ethic and a family-first lifestyle, but that my rest patterns are not what they should be. I'm constantly fighting to keep this right in me.

Earlier this year I was reading my Twitter® feed, probably at like 11 p.m., when I ran into this graphic on Fast Company® outlining the results of a study on sleep deprivation. [2] It warned of some of the direct consequences from a lack of rest. It said that when you don't get the appropriate levels of rest, you put yourself at risk for memory loss, low learning retention, less of a sex drive, increase in aging, greater risk for heart disease and various cancers, increase in weight gain, depression, and just plain grumpiness. Seriously, it sounds like Jesus was onto something. (I know; earth-shattering, isn't it?) This lack-of-rest thing is a strong rebuke to the do-more-and-more mindset in so many pastors and churches.

How about you? Is this part of your DNA, too? I mean, are you inclined like I am to do and do and do? If so, then maybe you and I need to schedule a rest. Seriously. Schedule it into your life and your ministry. I have had to put rest into my calendar and literally plan for it. I have to mark it as sacred and defend fiercely against the tendency in me to say yes to something that takes away what seems selfish for me. Doing nothing just doesn't do anything for my to-do list, my need to git-er-done, or my passion to live life to its fullest. But when I do honor it, it does everything to fuel my joy, my longevity, my presence, and my connection with Jesus. And if the studies are true, then it does everything to keep me healthy, alive, remembering important things, and living the good life, too.

CHAPTER SEVEN

SAFETY IS OVERRATED

FOR the last decade or so of youth ministry, I have annually taken young men to get away on a man trip with our high school ministry. The women go on their own with other female volunteers and staff to one location while the men all go with me to another. We've been to the snow, we've rented huge, crazy houseboats, and in the San Diego area, we've been to the desert for six years in a row. Our most recent trip again proved to be a great experience. We joined forces with another likeminded youth ministry from Orange County and took a lot of food, set up shooting ranges for shotguns and rifles, played paintball with slingshots, enjoyed massive bonfires, participated in great conversations, and took all kinds of risks together. Physically, mentally, spiritually, and emotionally, we tried to lead these young men into risk. We didn't do it recklessly, but we did try it intentionally.

Every year as we leave, I have to avoid the tendency to hear the moms' prayers for safety. As they drop off their sons, I hear them say, "OK, honey. Have fun. Be safe." I know what they mean: "Don't shoot yourself or your friends. Don't let something blow up in your face. I carried you for nine months in my belly, and I've poured into you for 13 years since then, so don't come back with all your parts in all the wrong places." I get it, and I also don't want hospital trips—especially not from the middle of nowhere. Danny, my friend who pastors the group from Orange County, told me that one mom from his church said to him, "I know my son is going to get hurt. So you don't need to call me. I'll see you when you get back and deal with it then." Amazing. What a contrast.

I don't really want to be a part of safe Christianity any more than I want to take a group of young men to the desert to have a tea party. I want them to be dangerous. I want to be dangerous. No, I'm not saying we should be the idiots of Christianity and lead these young men into stupid risk. But yes, I am sick of leading a boring, safe, predictable life. Who wants to follow Jesus into that? Look around; we don't need Jesus to do that. The fact is, routines in life will produce normalcy and are a deathblow to radical living. I think it's easy for my ministry, my family, and even my life to just go day-by-day with no sense of wonder or awe. To just do what is and has been expected is completely normal and intensely uninteresting.

We've probably all been told that we need to live like the Christians in Acts 2. We have networks of churches that rally around it as their goal. I've heard and taught several sermons on it. I even found a church online that calls itself the "acts2church," and its website claims they are the only one like it in the world.[3] That's a bold statement, to say the least. But this Acts 2 thing was radical. It is, quite honestly, largely foreign to the experience people have today in most churches. I have not seen a write-up in a magazine in a long time that looked like this or described life and faith like this in the local church:

They devoted themselves to the apostles' teaching and to fellowship, to the breaking of bread and to prayer. Everyone was filled with awe at the many wonders and signs performed by the apostles. All the believers were together and had everything in common. They sold property and possessions to give to anyone who had need. Every day they continued to meet together in the temple courts. They broke bread in their homes and ate together with glad and sincere hearts, praising God and enjoying the favor of all the people. And the Lord added to their number daily those who were being saved (Acts 2:42-47).

So I have two reactions to this call to be the Acts 2 church. One is defensive. I know this will not be met with a lot of agreement, but the truth is, I'm not called to be Acts 2. I'm called to be Acts 2012 (or insert your own year here, if you're reading this book a few years after it was published). I know that's subtle, but I think it's significant, too.

Interestingly you don't find Acts 2 behavior in Acts 10 either. By Acts 15, when Acts 2 and Acts 10 collide, Christians are fighting in Jerusalem over circumcision and whether Gentiles could be a part of this movement. The story is awesome, but it also is constantly changing as God moves. Perhaps God wants to work like this in all of us all the time, but for whatever reason, not every day is "epic." That was even true for Jesus. John reminds us in John 21:25 that Jesus did way more than the Gospels record, but for nearly two decades, Jesus just largely lived life among friends and family. And when he began to move into his public ministry after his baptism by John, some people said, "Isn't that the carpenter's son?" and "How can anything good come from Nazareth?"

The constant Christian guilt trip that says we should live every day crazy, selling all we have to help others and raising people from the dead is just not how life works. It's like guilting students for experiencing a spiritual high at summer camp. Who are we kidding? It's a spiritual high! Every day cannot be camp! Yes, it's an awesome window in time that should change us beyond camp. But every day cannot be this.

But my second reaction is to go on the offensive. OK, so maybe my church is not going to be just like Acts 2 all the time, but it also shouldn't be that radically different. There should be times from the last year when I've stopped and said, "Wow, that was a crazy 'God thing' that changed everything!" I mean, when did God stop wanting the church to be selfless or devoted or generous or miraculous? When did those things ever cease to be the call of God on the church? And here's the kicker: When did I ever decide to settle for less? If we're looking at our churches, families, and marriages and wondering where the risk went, then we usually have to look no further than the mirror to find our answer.

If I really want my church to be filled with Acts 2 people, then maybe I need to look at my own life and ask, "Am I an Acts 2 person?" Am I living dangerously and taking risks for the kingdom of God? Am I stockpiling stuff that won't last so I can acquire the latest gadgets, or am I selling stuff to help the poor? Really, when did the former start to trump the latter? When did our lives move out of Acts 2? I don't know really. But I do know that when my life moves into monotony, the things around me tend to move into predictability, too. When I stop taking risks, stop praying for the miraculous, and stop striving for what could and should be, then I find myself in a rut.

This really stared me straight in the face several years ago when Shannon and I were confronted with the opportunity for adoption. I say "confronted" because while it was on our radar, it was not the reason we went to Africa. My sister, Alisha, and her husband, Brad, had decided that God was calling them to Uganda for two years to serve with Engineering Ministries International. So in their own risk of faith, they sold or put everything they had in a garage and moved their family of five to Uganda. I followed by saying, "If you go, my family will come visit and we'll bring a missions team." The result was that they put us in touch with an orphanage to serve in, and we gathered a team and booked the flights.

Then one morning around 4 a.m., maybe three days into our stay in Uganda, while my wife could not sleep and was praying, she heard God. I know that sounds weird, because it doesn't happen every day for us either, but she heard God give her two names: "Becky and Billy." Neither of us knew who they were and neither of us had met them—until we found out that there were twins by those names at the orphanage. It's a crazy story and there's lot's more to it, but the bottom line is that I'd be lying to you if I said God miraculously telling my wife the names of two kids was a green light for me. It was not. It was a call to prayer but also a call to a serious evaluation of the kind of life I wanted to live.

I had good, God-honoring mentors in my life who encouraged me to adopt—and others who counseled me not to. Everyone realized my life was full already, and almost doubling our kid load from three to five didn't seem wise to many. Honestly, it made no sense to some. As much as we were motivated by a desire to not "pull a Jonah" and ignore God's clear call, the tipping point on the scales of life for me was this simple question: "What kind of life do I want to live?" It was clear this was risky. It was also clear to me that in our case, not doing it was not so much wise and safe as it was faithless and comfortable. If I wanted to model a radical life of faith for my family and ministry, it was time to put my life where my mouth was. It was time to follow the Lord into adoption.

If you, too, are mad at the lack of risk in your ministry or the lack of faith in your family or the lack of gutsy moves in your marriage, then look at the lack of risk in you first. Maybe it's time to sell something, pray something, or risk something radical for the kingdom of God, and invite your spouse, family, and ministry to join you. I'm praying you lead the way and invite those around you along for the risky ride of faith.

CHAPTER EIGHT

ME TIME

PERHAPS the most selfish-sounding concept in this book is that of "me time." Yes, I actually call it that. It's when I can focus on me. It's when I ditch the worries of ministry, the demands of my family, and the pressure of unfinished tasks to invest in my own heart, mind, body, and soul. Sometimes it takes the shape of going for a run or playing a game of indoor soccer. Sometimes it means sitting in solitude or quietly reading. Sometimes it means taking a nap. Sometimes it even means doing some task that's on my priority list and no one else's. It's like this thing I've wanted to do for forever, and today I'm going to say no to everyone else and do what has been bugging me, because it's my time.

It's all rooted in an understanding that a lack of "me time" affects everything and everyone around us. It means that when we get physically out of shape, our energy drains and we can't be present like we want to. When we fail to invite God to fill our souls in times of rest and solitude, then it's inevitable that a spiritually dry spell is on the horizon and our marriage, family, and ministry will feel its affects. That's the value of "me time," and in my experience, despite the high need for it, it's also ridiculously hard to justify, support, and protect in the midst of the increasing demands of marriage, family, and ministry.

When Shannon and I talked at that marriage retreat where I laid out the basic premises of this book, one of the biggest conclusions we reached was that we were not taking care of ourselves like we needed to. Even this retreat was evidence that we cared about our marriage and were making time for it. We valued the responsibility of being parents on a deep level and would often sacrifice time and work for our kids. But the one who was getting the short end of the stick was each of us. We were not prioritizing time to read, pray, exercise, or get away to tend to our own souls the way we ought to, and it was becoming evident in the things around us.

For me, this is particularly hard; because I am already away from the kids at work, it seems like every chance I have I should give more to my wife or kids. I come home after they have not seen me all day, and I feel the need to pour into them. They each need affection; my wife needs help and an adult conversation. The list goes on.

Additionally, one of my roles in our home is the morning routine. I make breakfast, help assemble lunches, and get the kids off to school on my way to work. This often means that if I want "me time" in the morning, I have to get up at like 5 a.m. This is a hard time because it feels forced and is not really a time I picked. If you're doing the math, then you've figured out that this means mornings are bad and evenings are full. So internally I wrestle with, "When do I get me time, and does anyone else even care?"

At our retreat, I discovered that this lack of focused time on my soul meant I was starting to give out of the depths of my bucket instead of the overflow of God in me. It was wearing on my patience and affecting my ability to extend grace to others. In Shannon's life, I found myself growing increasingly jealous of the "alone night" she was getting every Wednesday when our kids were watched by a college student as I went off to lead our high school small groups and Shannon got to go to a movie or just read at Starbucks® if she wanted. But from her perspective, it was one night a week in a full life of getting our monster family everywhere she needed. She didn't see it as fulfilling, but instead it was a slow drip to combat a constantly draining bucket. The result is that neither of us was getting this right and if our marriage was not going to be the blame zone, then we needed to rethink this value and prioritize setting aside some "me time."

We identified for each of us a need in our own lives that we needed the other to support. For Shannon, it was a weekend off. She wanted to leave the kids and go somewhere for two nights and sit. She wanted to go for a walk, sleep in, watch a movie, soak in a tub, get a pedicure, and not have to worry about making dinner—just have an extended time of no responsibility to refuel her soul so she could get centered. We looked at our calendar and decided on May as the best time for her to do this. I scoured the Internet for a deal and found her a place about 30 minutes away where she could pamper herself for three days. The honest truth was that it was easy to book and hard to support. Regardless of which of us was going away, it would cost us time and money, and it would force the other person to be a single parent so the spouse could be spoiled. If you don't place a high value on "me time" as the best investment you can make into "us time," then this experience will simply drive you insane and further embitter everyone around you.

For me, the biggest need beyond finding weekly space in my own life to just go for a run or read my blog roll was the need for accountable men that I could do life with. I already talked about this in an earlier chapter. But this was huge in the realm of taking care of me. For me, that four-day retreat represented stints of solitude, time to connect, time to pour into me and have others do the same. It was, and is to this day, a critical part of a healthy me. While that trip leaves my wife a single mom of five while I go off tending to my soul, we both have come to see the necessity for it.

Without a mutually owned and clear value on the need to take care of yourself, it will not happen. The truth is, the healthiest thing you can do for "we time" is get yourself some solid "me time."

CHAPTER NINE

IN SEARCH OF THE ME I'M CALLED TO BE

IN January 2009 I wrote this on my blog in a post entitled "Something is Broken."

> I'm not sure what just yet, but something's broken. Maybe in me. Maybe in my ministry. Maybe both. But it's clearly broken and I'm not sure how to fix it or even that there is one solution. I know of some things that are broken that I can and should fix. I know of other things that are broken that I think I could fix if someone holding that thing would just say, "OK, I agree it's broken. Let's fix it together." But this thing that is broken is deeper than either of those.

> I can't describe it or put my finger on "it," but I'm hunting. Tonight I walked into my house, and Shannon and I unanimously said, "What is that smell? Something is dead

in here." I'm not sure if a rat died in a wall or the milk is rotten in the fridge, but something is not right. I have that same feeling about several other things right now. "Something is dead in here."

…I don't know what it is, but I know something is broken and I can't fix it with my hammer, my computer, or by myself. I'm on a quest.

Can you identify with that? Have you ever had that sinking feeling like something is broken and you just don't know what it is? Like maybe something is rotten and it's time to empty the fridge to find the source? If so, then I'm with you. Don't ignore it. I think God is stirring in you.

In an effort to find the source of this discontent, I decided to start in my soul. I honestly didn't know if it was in my ministry, marriage, or family—but I thought I'd start in me. To do that, I needed some time and space, and I thought I knew a place where I could find both. At the time, Youth Specialties had its offices in my community and had just moved into this beautiful new and BIG workspace. It was a large warehouse-type industrial complex that had been turned into a giant open-forum office. No one on staff had private offices, and to compensate, they had worked hard to create several rooms for brainstorming and private conversations. Each room was designed differently, but often the spaces had entire walls covered in whiteboard paint to make a seemingly infinite brainstorming space with no parameters. I asked some friends if

I could camp out in a brainstorming room for two or three days to do some soul searching, and they said yes.

To do this, I started dumping everything from inside me onto a wall. I used pens, Sticky Notes®, and anything I could find to get it out. I stood in front of this blank wall and listed hopes, dreams, fears, to-do lists, stuff that stressed me out, and stuff that inspired me. I listed things I needed to do at home, places I wanted to go, things I wanted to do with my marriage, my family, and my ministry. I poured out everything I could find and every note I had buried in some "get it done" pile anywhere in my life. If I physically or emotionally carried it even slightly, I wrote it down.

It took a full day. When I was done, the entire wall was covered. I stood there looking at all that was inside and the huge space it took to hold it all when I spread it out, and I said, "No wonder I was stressed. That's a lot." It felt like when you have a mess in your garage that's so big you have no clue where to start. So instead of trying to work with it, you just start dragging everything you can put your hands on out into the driveway and spread it out everywhere. Then when you see it all, you can't believe it all fit in the garage in the first place. That's what I was feeling. It was both a relief to know it wasn't in there anymore and a bit overwhelming, and if I'm honest, it was embarrassing. Part of me wanted to just shove it back in the garage of my soul and ignore it so no one saw it.

But if I was going to address it and not ignore it, I had the difficult task of trying to figure out what to hold on to, what to chuck, and what to give away. I also had this sinking feeling that I couldn't do this on my own. So with my whole life on display, I cautiously invited a few people in. My wife came first. Before I walked her into this room, I told her it was my whole heart on a board and that she had to put away every knife and sharp object. It could be molded and carved, but spoons were all she could use. Just be gentle, I told her; I'm still bleeding from the surgery I already did. She graciously looked at the wall and, after some time of reading and taking it all in, said, "Wow, babe, that's a lot to keep in." I said, "I know. Can you gently tell me what you see?"

Through the next hour we processed some stuff together, named some things that I was carrying alone for her and our family that she thought were not worthy of keeping or being concerned with, and talked openly about where we had been and where we were headed. We prayed, and the next day I invited two mentors from the YS offices, Tic and Marko, to take a look and tell me what they saw. They, too, agreed that it was more than anyone should carry, and the overwhelming conclusion from both of them was that before I decided what to keep or chuck, I needed to decide who I was called to be. If I knew clearly *who I wanted to be*, I could then decide *what I wanted to do*.

Along the way, I realized I was having a bit of a midlife crisis. I tried to ask if I was content with who and what I had become thus far and seek God's plan for my future. I had moments of confession, conviction, and inspiration. In the process, I identified five main values I wanted to live into, some of which became shaping for this book. They were soul-shaping for me, and once identified, they were such a huge reminder and driver for the life I wanted to live. The next few pages reveal my conclusions. They may be helpful for you. But more than my conclusions, maybe the truth is you need to do your own assessment. Maybe the greatest gift you could give yourself and those around you is a clear understanding of who God is calling you to be.

BRIAN'S FIVE LIFE VALUES:

PLEASE GOD, NOT PEOPLE (Galatians 1:10; Colossians 3:23-24; Jeremiah 9:23-24)

- Guard my heart from the things that will destroy it. (Proverbs 4:23)

- Remain broken so God won't have to break me. (Psalm 51:17)

- Live for God, regardless of the choices of others. (Genesis 6:9; Job 1:8)

- Be a passionate follower of Jesus. (Romans 12:11)

TAKE CARE OF MY SOUL AND MY FAMILY BEFORE MY MINISTRY (1 Timothy 3:4-5)

- Maintain sustainable and healthy life rhythms—food, exercise, rest, work, play, and so on.

- Maximize the ministry of the moment.

- Invest intentional time in my marriage and kids. Be with them and for them.

    - The best gift I can give my marriage is a God-honoring, healthy me.

    - The best gift I can give my kids is a God-honoring, healthy marriage.

    - The best gift I can give my ministry and community is a God-honoring, healthy family.

BE A LEARNER

- There are only two ways to learn things: the hard way and from those who learned it the hard way. Choose the latter.

- Humility is the defining ingredient of godly leadership, so seek it. (Philippians 2:3-8)

- Spend time in environments that will stretch and grow me.

- Admit and own my failures.

- Ask good questions.

- Seek out mentors.

BE INTENTIONAL ABOUT MY DECISIONS

- Say yes and no on purpose, seeking counsel and thinking big picture.

- Do what I love. Build a team that includes those who love to do what drains me.

- Decide which is truer: (A) If I don't, others won't, OR (B) Because I do, others don't.

- Personal discipline cannot be delegated to, purchased from, or found in others. It is my job and must be Holy Spirit-driven.

WORK HARD TO BE AND DO THE THINGS GOD HAS CALLED ME TO

- If it's not worth doing right, it's not worth doing. (1 John 2:6; 2 Timothy 4:5-8; 1 Corinthians 9:23-27)

- Empower others.

- Invite a generation to understand, own, and live out a life-changing faith in Jesus.

- Teach students how to think, not what to think.

- Provide opportunities for students to fail safely.

- Develop my teaching gifts to level of mastery.

- Train and mentor others—especially in youth ministry (via my writing, one-on-one convos, and teaching/training opportunities).

- Be a leader and vision caster.

SECTION TWO

THE BEST GIFT I CAN GIVE MY FAMILY IS A HEALTHY MARRIAGE

We have a big Lab/Rottweiler mix puppy named Zeus. OK, he's probably not a puppy anymore, but we call him a puppy. He's like 115 pounds of craziness, so his actions say puppy but his body says brute. He essentially looks like a Lab, but he has broad shoulders and a big head like his mom, who was a full-blood Rottweiler. He likes to run and play and chase the wild rabbits that live in our community.

We love our puppy, but there are several things we have done to keep him happy and healthy that don't make much sense from my perspective. One is that we only feed him two cups of dry food twice a day. Whenever we feed him, he acts like he could eat 50 times that much, and I swear, if I put it in front of him he would. He's like a kid who will eat himself sick if you hand him a big bag of candy. He has zero portion control, so to keep him healthy we have to do this for him.

Secondly, we have "kennel trained" him. This means when we leave, instead of giving him the run of the yard or the roam of the house, we simply say, "Kennel" and he runs to a dog-sized cage in the corner and lies down and falls asleep. What is crazy to me is that when we leave for the day and I take him outside to go to the bathroom, I have to coax him to come because he is afraid I'll leave him outside and not in his kennel. He'd evidently much rather be safe in there than out defending the yard all day against those evil people walking their own dogs on our street, which seems to be his other favorite activity after chasing rabbits.

I say all of this because when I think about marriage and the needs of my kids, no, I don't think about my dog. But I do think that the things that seem the most natural to me are not the most needed. Zeus needs lots of food and lots of exercise, so logic says don't limit his portions or put him in a kennel. But my experience and my vet say that's not right. The truth is, I can't just respond to my dog's demands as they arise. Instead, I have to do what is counterintuitive.

Similarly, my kids need lots of love, support, and attention, and for what it's worth, my ministry has an endless list of needs, too. Both my kids and my ministry, therefore, have an insatiable demand on my life. No matter what I do, I never manage to spend enough time or money to meet all their needs. And therefore, it would seem that if I want to take care of my kids, I should do more with my kids. If I want to take care of ministry, then I should go to a student's game and watch in the stands. These are not inherently wrong, but they are not actually the first things I should do. Perhaps they can't be ignored and maybe they are even real needs, but they are not the primary need.

The most important thing I can do for my kids and even my ministry is to pour into my marriage first. Put another way, the best thing that I can do for my kids is to love their mom. Think about it. If my marriage falls apart, so will my family and my ministry. There's no two ways around that. We all could list both national and personal examples, both inside and outside of the church, to prove this point. When marriage falls apart, life falls apart. Period.

The integrity of my family (and my ministry by default of it being downstream) rests firmly on the foundation of my marriage, which is composed of two people who cannot expect that it is anyone's job to fix them. Like we have already talked about, a healthy marriage is made from a healthy me, and I can't expect my marriage to fix me. The health of my heart and soul is my responsibility, and it radically affects my marriage and everything else. In the same way, though, I can't expect my family or my ministry to fix my marriage. It is a one-way street. When my marriage is a mess, so is everything else. I'm not talking about the old adage of "happy wife, happy life" or "happy spouse, happy house." Happy isn't always the goal. What I am saying is that if we want to radically bless our families in a healthy way, then the very best thing that we can do for them is love our spouse.

Ephesians 5 contains a passage that is often quoted in marriage seminars and weddings. Sometimes it's used sarcastically and poorly in contexts where some chauvinist is trying to keep a woman "in her place" by telling her to submit to her husband. But these are arrogant comments rooted in bad hermeneutics that ignore the context of the passage, not the least of which is verse 21: *Submit to one another out of reverence for Christ.* Submission is not a one-way street; it is a two-way street. It requires two people mutually and personally submitted to Jesus who then mutually and personally submit to one another. If you get the order wrong at any point, you'll get marriage wrong, too. If you submit to a husband or a wife before you submit your own life to Jesus, you'll end up angry and bitter at your spouse.

You'll start blaming your spouse for your problems. If you submit your marriage to the demands of your kids before you do to one another, you'll end up serving your kids and not your spouse. Submission has an order to it that is God-ordained. It is Jesus first and it is mutual and it is how a healthy marriage grows.

Just like Zeus finds great contentment in the shelter of his kennel, my family will find great contentment in the shelter of my marriage. My kids don't just need the freedom to run; they need the confidence to know that when they do, our home is a safe place to return to. When my kids know that their mom and dad are in love, faithful to one another, devoted to God, and predictably there for them, their hearts are at ease. Every time I put my marriage at risk or serve someone else outside of the context of our mutual submission to Jesus and one another, I put my whole world at risk.

If you want to love your kids, then love your spouse. If that priority is out of whack, then stop and get it right. Don't assume it will be OK or heal over time. Get help. Get focused. Get it right. Your marriage is your calling from God. It is more powerful than your family and your ministry ever will be because both are flowing downstream out of it.

CHAPTER TEN

HEY ROOMMATE... WANNA PAY THE BILLS?

WHEN I went to college, I lived with a group of roommates. In fact, it was never just two guys in a dorm-room scenario. Instead we always had at least three bedrooms and one common space in an apartment-type living situation. The first two years we lived on campus and the last two we lived off campus. As a result, I never lived with fewer than five guys sharing a space—and sometimes it was as many as eight of us. We had common living rooms, split some of the bills, and shared the cleaning. We were roommates not so much because we wanted to experience communal living, but mainly because none of us could afford to live alone.

Because I grew up with my parents and just my one younger sister, I'd always had my own room. So living in a space with a bunch of guys was, at times, a bit challenging for my own personal space issues, especially in the bathroom when you'd be showering and some guy would come stink the place up—and locking the door stopped no one. Truth be told, four years of living like this ran all my space and modesty issues right out of me. All in all, the roommate season of my life was filled with amazing memories, late-night craziness, shared adventures, and tons of bonding. But it was a season. While we all loved our days in Davis, none of us had any dreams of being roommates forever, and almost all of us are now married and living life somewhere else.

Every once in a while, my wife and I find ourselves slipping into the college dorm lifestyle. When we do, we call it "roommate mode." No, this doesn't mean we start having keggers on Thursdays, staying up too late, leaving empty pizza boxes on the floor, and having sex in any available twin bed. That would be way more interesting and would be called something else. What it does mean is that we stop focusing on each other and become people who simply share a space and not our lives. It means we evidently walked the aisle so that we could split the bills, get a tax deduction, and share the chores. It means that our marriage is no longer about loving one another or creative dating or even significant conversations. Instead, all we talk about is what bills are due, what kid needs to be where, and what project needs to be added to the to-do list.

That's roommate mode, and it is deadly to a healthy marriage. If you're in it, admit it to each other and get out of it. Call a sitter and go on a date. If you have school-age kids, then skip the sitter and take the morning off. Ban the bills, the kids, the chores, and the church from your discussion. Just talk about you. What do you love? How are you doing? What are your fears and joys and needs? Make the time to fall in love again and remind yourselves that marriage is way too significant to be downgraded to common living partners who get tasks done.

If you need to, make a sign: "SAY NO TO ROOMMATE MODE!" Then stick it on your computer screen or hang it over the washing machine, the kitchen sink, or the front door. Just don't let the pressure of raising kids and a mounting to-do list rob you of the adventure that moved you two to say yes to marriage and to walk the aisle to spend the rest of your lives together.

CHAPTER ELEVEN

WHOSE LANGUAGE ARE YOU SPEAKING?

AROUND the time of the infamous seven-year mark in marriage, my wife and I hit a really tough spot. I remember driving in December to a family vacation with my parents and my sister's family in Lake Tahoe, and while the kids slept, my wife and I fought. Ministry was demanding, family was expanding, and we were not doing well. We had passed roommate mode and entered something much more severe. We were trying to figure out if we needed counseling or what, and something clearly had to change.

In the aftermath of that day, somehow my wife stumbled across the book *The 5 Love Languages* by Gary Chapman. In it he outlines that we all have basically five filters or languages through which we give and receive love. Without going into too much detail, he says that we tell others we love them in one of several ways:

- giving gifts and showering someone with stuff you make or buy for them

- serving and helping them do things we know how to do

- physically touching with hugs and kisses and affection

- sharing words, telling them, and writing encouraging notes

- spending time together, showing the other that they are a priority

If you've read the book, then you know what these are and how to identify them. But because we had not, for us, these were revolutionary. As we read, we began to discover that we would say that we loved each other in different ways. Because neither of us had language for it, all we knew was that we were loving the other but the other person was not loving back. Shannon identified her love languages as "time spent" and "words of affirmation" and mine were "serving" and "physical touch."

As we began to talk about the implications of these love languages, all kinds of things came into clarity. On a Saturday, it was not uncommon for me to go outside and wash the car, mow the lawn, weed the plants, and spend a large amount of my day serving my wife. I expected that as I did these things for her, she felt good about her house, enjoyed driving a nice clean car, and the whole time was thankful for my devotion to our marriage. However, my wife's love languages aren't the same as mine, so my "serving in love" meant that the entire day I was spending no time with her and no words were coming her way because we were apart.

In addition, it was not uncommon for me to be thinking, "I'm doing a lot of work out here. Sure would be nice if Shannon would come help me and then we could go do something together." About the same time Shannon would be thinking, "Sure would be nice if Brian would hire a gardener or let me get the car washed on the corner so that we could spend the day together instead of doing chores. Doesn't he love me?"

When we did bring up these issues, it usually would end with something like Shannon rather annoyed and asking me where I'd been all day. I'd tell her what I'd been doing, expecting to be met with praise and affection. Instead, I was met with confusion and frustration. I would then say something fabulous like, "Well, you should have married a rich guy" and then that would be the end of it.

But once we had language for our communication, we had a way to not only give but also to receive love more clearly. Sitting around watching TV with my wife was, to me, a waste of time. I'm not a big TV fan. But for my wife, it was time spent. Even doing two separate things in the same room, for her, was time together. This was both crazy and refreshing to me. I figured out that if I canceled something at church to spend time with my wife, it was like the grand slam of love. I even started putting stuff on the calendar that I never intended to do, just so I could cancel events and be with her. (Ha! Just kidding—but I should try that!) Anyway, I was being given new information on how to love Shannon in a way that she could receive, and in the same way, she was given a new lens through which to receive my love.

A few years after this love language discovery on our part, we decided to do a HUGE home remodel. It actually involved the complete redo of about 50 percent of our house, including two bathrooms and the kitchen. Because it was so significant and because we did not have a ton of money to pay someone else to do it, we decided to move our family out while the project was under way. Essentially I would camp in our home for a month while my wife and kids lived at grandma's. To pull it off, I decided I'd work at church for two or three days a week and on our home the remaining four days.

I remember getting done with the plan and sitting down at the table for one final conversation with Shannon before starting the long purchase-and-supply list. I told her that during this entire month, she'd have few words and little time spent with me, often going days without much connection. The reason would be because I'd be serving our family and loving her by giving her a nicer home to live in. But I also said that at the end of this project, if she came into the house to a brand-new space that I'd busted my rear to make for her and she just wondered where I'd been all month, I was gonna blow a gasket. This project was going to require a month of misses in Love Language 101, and we needed to go into it with our eyes wide open. I was not willing to go back to our Tahoe car ride again, and if my failure to speak my wife's love language was only going to be a 30-day drain on her love tank, then I would rather keep the nasty bathrooms and skip the remodel altogether. With that understanding, we moved forward and ended up with a nicer home and a healthier marriage at the same time. Just a couple of years earlier, it would not have ended that way.

So what about you? Are you and your spouse speaking the same language? Are you working hard to tell your spouse you love them in ways that they understand and to hear it in ways they are wired to show it? If you need to, go buy Chapman's book. It's cheaper than counseling and might save you a ton of headaches.

CHAPTER TWELVE

GUILT TRIP DATING

YOU should have a weekly date night. The fact that you don't is evidence that you don't love Jesus or your spouse—and that you probably kick puppies for fun. You'll never ever be invited to mentor a newlywed couple or lead a married Bible study because you're a loser. Everyone knows that a healthy marriage holds a weekly date night as holy, and only a fool wouldn't do it. You and 10 other couples on the planet are the only ones who don't do this.

Ever felt like that? If not, good job; so glad you have a date night. Skip this chapter. But if you do feel this way, let me tell you about our journey in this area.

For years, Shannon and I had to find creative ways to steal a date. It was really a non-issue when we didn't have kids. I remember one night when our house was super hot; we had no AC and neither of us could sleep. So I asked, "You awake?" Shannon said, "Yup" in a voice that made it sound like she'd been awake as long as I had and was just as sick of it. Because it was around midnight, I said, "Wanna go to Walmart®?" (I know; I'm a romantic genius.) But much to my surprise she said, "Yup." So we went and bought a ceiling fan and ice cream. I stayed up until 3 a.m. assembling the dumb fan—probably due to a combination of the fact that it was cheap and that I was half-awake at this point. It was fun and ridiculous, but totally doable with no kids.

Then came the kids, and dating got more complicated. Not only were financial demands getting tighter with the introduction of diapers and the 4,000 other things babies "need" in the U.S., but our time was getting harder to steal away, too. The result was that the simple date night was not so simple anymore, and dating the old-fashioned way was just not in the budget. If we could get the grandparents to help, we were set. But if we hired a babysitter, a four-hour dinner-and-movie date could easily cost us $80 to $100. We simply didn't have the money. So we had to get creative, which often meant a "date breakfast." In our situation, Shannon was not trying to do mom duty while working another job, so we could drop the kids off at preschool and then grab a couple of hours or so together in a coffee shop.

When the kids all hit grade school and Shannon started teaching as a substitute again, we had to manipulate our schedule around both her work and the church. But when we did, we could now spend the whole date eating, talking, and doing some basic life stuff together, too. It was complicated, but dating was also way cheaper in the daytime. If you're in a two-income family and both working days, then dating on a budget might mean ordering a meal delivered and grabbing a streaming movie on the couch after the kids are in bed. This is our first year with a kid in high school, so we can now "hire" our own son—which usually means we pay for his movie with his friends in exchange for him watching his brothers and sister while we go get sushi.

I could write for days trying to list all the possible "yeah but what about" scenarios of couples and dating. Everything from split work shifts to blended families to dating in a military family—they all require another level of consideration and planning. No two families' scenarios are the same. But regardless of what yours is like, I think it's important to decide three things.

1. Decide that you will not succumb to the dating guilt trip. When you date your spouse, don't do it to silence critics who claim to know how and what is the right thing to do. Instead, do it to honor your marriage.

2. Second, do date. Find a creative way for you as a couple to get together. Date over breakfast, a long lunch break, or on some weeknight. Just don't dismiss it as too hard to pull off. Redefine the date, turn off your work cell phone, and invest in your marriage.

3. Do plan to get away without the kids from time to time.

I know a couple who recently went on their first kid-free vacation in 20 years. Seriously, for 20 years they never took a weekend or a week to go be a couple again. I can't imagine doing that. I know it's all but impossible with newborns, but 20 years? Wow. Maybe one of the reasons the weekly date night babysitter cost too much for us was the priority we placed on the semi-annual getaway weekend. For the entirety of our marriage, Shannon and I have gotten away once in November for her birthday and once in June for our anniversary. Sometimes we managed to score a vacation home from someone in our church who would lend it to us. Sometimes we would save up and pay for it. We always had to arrange childcare or family for the kids to stay with; occasionally several families would help.

It was never easy, but those three days and two nights away have been and remain critical times for us to get away and invest in our marriage. Just like a weekly youth group meeting will never replace the value of a good weekend retreat, a weekly date will never replace the value of a getaway retreat with your spouse, either. There's just something radically different about extended, uninterrupted time together. Go camping. Go stay in a hotel. Borrow a vacation rental. Do a "stay-cation" and farm the kids out so you have three days of uninterrupted "you time" where you vow to sleep in and do no chores. Do whatever your budget can afford—just don't skip it.

Ditch the guilt trip; just don't ditch dating.

CHAPTER THIRTEEN

I DIDN'T SIGN UP FOR THIS

EVERYBODY signs up for stuff they didn't sign up for.

When I signed up to be a soccer coach, I knew I was signing up to teach the skills and rules necessary for competition, to run practice, and to create a game plan. What I didn't know was that I also signed up to be the parent manager, the volunteer-getter for the fundraiser, the communicator of scores to five other people, the end-of-season party planner, the goal setter-upper/ taker-downer, and the banner man. Wow, I signed up for a lot.

If you've ever signed papers to buy a house, then you know this feeling, too. You sign up to buy a house but then discover that you actually signed up to buy it for A LOT more than you thought you did because they make you sign that one page where they spell out all the interest you're paying, too. Then when your water main breaks or your roof leaks, you realize that you signed up to be a home repairperson, too. Oh, and when the property taxes come, you find out that you signed up to pay that, too—and the list goes on.

If you've been doing youth ministry for any length of time at all, you've figured out there was quite a bit of fine print in the job description that no one told you about, either. Trash picker-upper, letter or recommendation writer, Facebook master, mission trip travel agent, and car locksmith rarely make the official list.

This truth is like a promise of life or something—and there is no job or decision that seems to be immune to it. But the problem is actually not that signing up for stuff signs you up for stuff you didn't sign up for. (Go ahead; read that sentence again.) It's inevitable. The real problem is when the thing you didn't sign up for takes priority over the thing you did sign up for. That's the real danger.

One time Shannon and I were away on retreat with our church staff in Palm Springs, California, at the Westin®. (I know, tough day on the job. Ministry is always hard.) Anyway, one morning we woke up and saw this card shoved under our hotel door that said if we went to a one-hour presentation in the afternoon, we'd get free breakfast at this buffet that cost around $30 per person, along with a $50 gift certificate to spend in their shops. We decided to burn an hour of our free time on Saturday and go to this presentation to score a nice free breakfast on our last day and buy something nice for Shannon's mom, who was watching the kids. Seemed innocent enough; how bad could it be?

But, oh were we wrong! If you've ever been to a time-share presentation, you know it's like the travel sales version of a store that makes you walk a certain path to get to the checkout stand. You know, one of those places like IKEA® that forces you to walk the whole store before you can buy one thing in the hopes that you'll buy 12 things instead. So after the beautiful and picturesque one-hour presentation, you sit down with a counselor who tries to get you to sign up for their program today. Right now. They work on commission and make it sound simple. "Just sign here," they say, "and you get XYZ, and it'll be so cheap you will hardly know you bought it. Plus, it's awesome and we have a payment plan for every budget."

But we were determined to not buy a thing. We told the gal flat out that we just wanted breakfast and a gift card. But she wouldn't give it to us until we paid for it with a high-pressure sales pitch. So we left feeling horrible and having lost about 90 minutes of our getaway weekend we could never get back. I would have rather paid for an overpriced breakfast than endured that.

About six months after kid No. 3 arrived, I remember feeling the same way. Shannon and I had been married for about eight years, and my wife had just given birth to our third child. Don't get me wrong, I loved and love my kids—all of them. But I started doing the math and realized that if you added it up, my wife had been pregnant or nursing a kid for more of our marriage than not. I had this heart attack that we were becoming the Duggars—you know, that TV family where the mom is like a baby machine and she's been pregnant pretty much for 20 years straight and she can now give birth while making breakfast. This is ironic now that we have five kids. God is funny like that. But at the time, I remember getting all defensive on my kids. It was like I woke up one morning and I realized that I lost my wife but they gained a mom.

I didn't sign up for this. We didn't sign up for this.

Sure, when Shannon and I were dating, then engaged, and then married, we talked about one day having kids. But we didn't get married so we could have kids. Marriage was a necessary first step, but kids were not the reason that we got married. It wasn't like I popped the question and said, "Will you marry me and have kids?" What I actually said was this: "Proverbs 18:22 says, 'He who finds a wife finds what is good and receives favor from the Lord.' Will you marry me?" She said yes, and we got married because we were in love and wanted to do life together with Jesus. But somewhere along the way, marriage had given way to parenthood, and our primary responsibility had subtly shifted to raising kids, not loving each other.

When nursing, my wife had each of our boys on a schedule. She was not a fan of the nurse-on-demand plan and decided, after reading a book on the topic, that she was going to tell our kids when to eat, not vice versa. Eventually, it would be like clockwork and she could plan her life around feeding and nap time, because it was a well-regimented machine and the boys' bodies just fell in line. At this point, I was feeling like it was time to do this with our marriage, too. It was time to declare some boundaries on when she was mom and when she was my wife. We started trying to declare certain conversations uninterruptible by children. I would come home and it would be kid time until dinner, and then after dinner, they would have to play on their own before showers because it was mom and dad's half-hour to be married.

I know of several marriages that have actually ended in divorce when their children reached their 20s because the entire marriage had revolved around raising kids. That's it. Once the kids were out of the house and mom and dad were "empty nesters," that term took on a double meaning. Their nest truly was empty. It was empty of kids, but it was also empty of connection, purpose, love, and relationship. They had stopped being married and had become a childrearing machine. In the process, they found themselves essentially permanent roommates, and because they didn't sign up for that, they signed out in divorce.

So how about you? Did you sign up for the marriage you're living? If not, it's time to rethink some stuff and remind yourself that the best gift you can give your kids is not whatever they want, but the marriage they don't know that they desperately need you to have.

CHAPTER FOURTEEN

MARRIAGE IN THE TEAKETTLE

YOU'VE likely heard of the experiment: When you put a frog in hot water, it will immediately find a way to jump out to save its life. But if you put that same frog in cold water and slowly raise it to a boil, it will sit there until it is boiled to death. I've never tried this with any frogs, but I believe it is true. Plenty of marriages die this way, too. I bet you can cite specific examples. I know I can, and sadly, I've had a front row seat to several of them.

No one wakes up one day married to a job; they slowly move themselves there one workday at a time. No one dives into the deep water of an affair in a one-night stand; they mentally and physically flirt their way there. No one just falls out of shape; they do it one meal and one lack of activity at a time. And in marriage, no one just stops listening to marital warning signs either; they just methodically roll over enough relational speed bumps until eventually a once-bad pattern is now normal.

In these cases, it's not the devil with horns, fire, and a pitchfork we need to watch out for. It's the wolf in sheep's clothing. It's the masquerading angel of light (see 2 Corinthians 11:14). *Be alert and of sober mind. Your enemy the devil prowls around like a roaring lion looking for someone to devour (1 Peter 5:8).* People in some marriages—maybe all marriages—need to sober their minds and open their eyes. The devil is on the prowl, and many of us are slowly moving into vulnerability.

There is a fine line between deciding you'll never have an affair and thinking you're not capable of it. The same is true of those who say, "We'll never get a divorce." While that may be the reality, that doesn't mean that you're married. Plenty of "married people" lead a life of divorce. Maybe they still have the same rings, joint bank accounts, and roof over their head, but their hearts are far from each other.

My grandparents grew up in a generation where you did not get a divorce. So they never did. But practically, they began to slowly live like it. They stopped vacationing together. They stopped being physically affectionate. They stopped sharing dreams and often complained about the other's agenda. As much as I could tell, they were loyal to one another, but they were not a unit. I never saw either set of my grandparents in the same bedroom. I rarely saw them kiss. They told me they "loved each other" and they had the rings and shared rooftop to prove it. But that was it.

If you asked me if I hope one day to stop sharing a bed with my wife, I would tell you that it's not on my agenda. Neither is divorce. But my experience and observation say that what you ignore can kill you. Deciding we will not have an affair or will not get divorced is NOT enough. If I don't follow that declaration with daily decisions, I'm doomed to subtly find myself living the very thing I want to avoid.

Maybe there's a solid list of the top ways to avoid this in your marriage. I'm sure we could spend some time and list them, but let me suggest one that might not make the normal list: Give your spouse "first right of refusal." I'll explain what I mean.

I think that in ministry, the marriages I've seen fall apart do so for one of two subtle reasons: The person has an affair either with the church or with someone at the church. I describe these as subtle reasons because I've never met a single soul who took a job at a church for this purpose. Despite this, I also know lots of people who have done both. I have a good friend whose wife once took and then had framed a picture of him walking out the door. She then put it on the mantle of their fireplace. At the time he was working two jobs, one as a landscape contractor and the other as the "part-time" youth pastor. Weeks went by and he never noticed it, but then one day he did. He asked his wife, "What is that? Why is that picture of me on the mantle?" She said, "Oh, I would have put your face on there, but I wanted to make sure your kids recognized you." Ouch! I'm not suggesting you do this, but she made her point loud and clear.

I'd be lying to you if I didn't tell you that my wife and I have had similarly tough talks in our own marriage. There was no picture on the mantle, but the topic was the same. In our marriage, the chief culprit of the church life affair is death by super-calendar. There's just too much to do and too many times when we agree to do it. A free night is given away to a meeting. A family function is bumped to adjust for some church "emergency." A summer calendar is planned and then family works around it.

To avoid this tendency, Shannon and I have agreed that she has first right of refusal. Sure, there are "normal things" that we both know are part of my job. Ministry is not a 9-to-5 calling. However, it is one where I can set much of my own schedule. So instead of picking a calendar or a meeting or taking an outside speaking or writing assignment by myself, we talk together about the implications on family, time, budget, and marriage. Shannon knows that she has veto power. To her credit, she doesn't exercise that veto at every turn, and I've worked hard not to put her in that position, even vetoing things before she has to. But when it is said, I honor it.

This means that at times I end up not pleasing even those I "answer to" at church. It means missing meetings and saying no to opportunities that will cost my marriage or family too much. It often means that I have to tell someone, "I'm sorry, but I can't meet with you this week; the calendar is at max capacity already, and we either have to connect another way or another time altogether." Protecting my marriage from the subtle drain of ministry demand is not something I can assume will happen. I have to be very proactive about it.

In a similar vein, I know several marriages that have been destroyed by an affair with another person, and all of them started casually. It was a glance, a flirting comment, a love note, a single tantalizing thought that over time led to a huge regret. Some caught themselves after a few months. Others went on for years. But all had tragic consequences.

I work with a staff of adult volunteers and students, often in close proximity. Sometimes people openly share their hearts, fears, and regrets in vulnerable moments when we are literally ministering on a soul level. Sometimes we spend hours working together on a project. These and other circumstances mean there are plenty of opportunities for an inappropriate relationship to develop. Yes, I enforce several personal barriers, such as choosing not to meet in private with other women, avoiding conversations that involve sexual integrity, and referring long-term needs to another woman or professional counselor. My appointment calendar is online and open to be viewed by my admin, my boss, and my wife.

But beyond that, I have also given my wife full access and disclosure in this area. Shannon doesn't currently serve in my high school program weekly, but she does come around often. In the process, if she doesn't like the mannerisms of a student around me or the way a woman looks at me, she knows she can quietly say so. And I fully honor her concern. Again, my wife is not paranoid and constantly telling me I can't speak to other women. But she is discerning, and I yield every time to her on this. I can only think of like three or four times in almost 20 years of ministry when she has said this, but when she has, I take a step back—so much so, that I'll even move to being cold with someone, if need be.

In the closest situation I've ever been to a marriage destroyed by a real affair, both parties actually had their spouses alert them of their fear and discontent with the relationship—and both individuals fully ignored that caution. I've watched the effects it has had on family, friendships, ministry, and even finances, and quite frankly, it scares me to death. It is NOT worth it. If you're in a relationship that is subtly and slowly moving toward marriage-like soul connection and intimacy, STOP. Give your spouse access to these relationships and move away from them.

This chapter is not a judgment. But it is a warning. What you and I don't think about can kill us. Is your marriage in a teakettle? If so, turn off the heat before it's too late.

CHAPTER FIFTEEN

THE MYTH OF BALANCE

"**IF** you loved God, you'd spend at least as much time reading your Bible as you do showering." Ever heard someone say something like that? Have you ever said it? The assumption is that the person who spends more time each day showering than reading the Bible cares more about vanity than about God. Maybe there's a sliver of truth in there, but the lie is that there's a one-to-one ratio between the amount of time something takes and the value you place on it. So if you spend four hours fixing your car and only 20 minutes reading your Bible, you care more about your car than you do about God. To fix this, you need to spend another three hours and 40 minutes reading your Bible. Applied to marriage it means if you spend eight hours a day at work and two hours a day with your spouse, you don't love your spouse as much as you love your job.

Let's take this model even further. I only see my parents around five times a year, but I see the person who cuts my hair every two weeks. This means I love my hairdresser more than my parents? No offense to my local $8 haircut shop, but that's absurd. People who hold to this model find themselves constantly in pursuit of "balance" in their lives by trying to place equal time and money in every bucket—and it's exhausting.

My mom used to do this with my sister and I at Christmas. She would methodically count up how much she spent and even how many packages we each had and make sure they matched almost exactly—to make sure her affection was balanced in its display. If it didn't work out and one of us got something that was costlier and therefore fit in fewer boxes, she would either go out of her way to make sure you knew why or just add a card with the difference in money to the other person's present to make it right.

She did this for years, and my sister and I never thought much of it—until we started having kids and it got really complicated. We had to tell our mom that we love her and her generosity, but that no one else is keeping a record and she doesn't have to either. When she and my dad fly to my sister's house and visit, I don't tally up the number of times or project the cost and then start making sure they give our family the same investment. Maybe I don't have to do that because my parents are intensely concerned about splitting their time with all their kids and grandkids. I have great parents and we know we are loved. But I also don't do it because I don't think that's what balance is. Balance—especially in marriage, family, and ministry—is not like balancing a scale with equal weight in every place. That is an impossible, stressful, and list-making way to manage one's life.

I knew this to be true, but I really had no language for this until August 2006 when I heard Wayne Cordeiro speak at the Global Leadership Summit, held at Willow Creek Church near Chicago. I was sitting in my church in San Diego watching this man teach via satellite when he started to talk about the impossibility of balance. He talked about the chasing he'd been doing and even the complete emotional breakdown he experienced while pastoring his huge congregation in Honolulu and trying to find the ever-elusive "balance." Finally, in an effort to avoid a complete mental breakdown, he unplugged his life and put himself in a monastery for solitude and a ministry stress detox. That's where he had this "aha" moment and realized balance is not about equal time in equal places. He said it's about moving the fulcrum.

Imagine that you had a classic old-world grain scale—the one with a pivot point in the middle of a bar with two plates hanging from chains on either side. Now imagine that your marriage is on one side and your ministry is on the other. Trying to constantly manage time and pressure in both, to make sure you have balance, is complicated in this model. If you were to make the scale more realistic, you'd need one that has like 5 or 10 plates on each side, labeling one for work, one for each kid in your family, one for your spouse, one for you, and one for all kinds of demands that you manage.

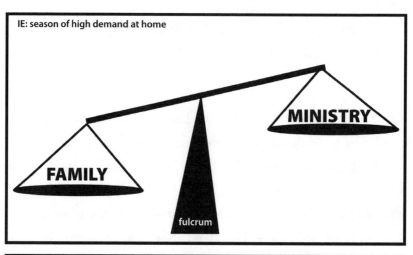

IE: season of high demand at home

FAMILY

MINISTRY

fulcrum

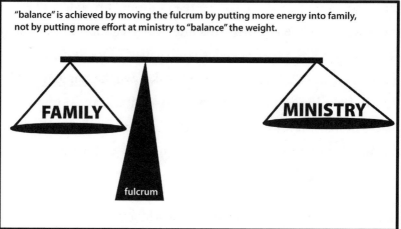

"balance" is achieved by moving the fulcrum by putting more energy into family, not by putting more effort at ministry to "balance" the weight.

FAMILY

MINISTRY

fulcrum

But this balancing of plates is impossible; it doesn't work. Maybe this is what Solomon had in mind when he wrote the long list of things that there's a time for, in Ecclesiastes 3—not simply two things to "balance," but rather 28 different things that each has its own time. *There is a time for everything, and a season for every activity under the heavens (Ecclesiastes 3:1).* Along these lines, what Cordeiro said was revolutionary for my life and mental peace. He said the way you find balance is not by giving a bunch of your time to one thing and then to trying to find a way to give a bunch of equal time to the other thing. Instead, you move the fulcrum.

So in the traditional balance model, if your spouse gets sick or if you go away for a weekend retreat, you're going to have way more weight on your marriage than on your work because the scale will tip and things will not be balanced anymore. Instead, just move the fulcrum of your life. You do this when you realize this is a season in which your marriage gets more of you, and you make no apologies for it. You will spend more time at home than at work this week because the weight of your life requires it. Likewise, there are seasons in ministry where the fulcrum will have to move the other direction—like the week before and the week of summer camp, maybe the fall kickoff, maybe Easter or Christmas, or maybe when someone in your church dies. These all require a fulcrum adjustment. You and your spouse have to look each other in the face and say, "I have to move the fulcrum."

This doesn't mean that you can keep the fulcrum in one place in your life or constantly justify it one direction and label that "balanced." But it does mean that sometimes you'll spend an inordinate amount of time on you, and that's OK. Sometimes it will be your marriage. Sometimes it will be your ministry. Balance becomes less about making sure everyone gets equal everything and more about making sure your fulcrum is actually moving.

For Shannon and I, the pressure this places on us is largely in the area of communication. When we talk honestly about our calendar and the demands of ministry and marriage, we do this well. When we don't move the fulcrum, someone is upset and feels cheated. This was huge for us during our adoption process because we were literally out of the country for 30 days. It was a 100-percent fulcrum move in the direction of marriage and family for weeks.

Most recently, this has come to bear on us because our wedding anniversary is June 25. Summer camp for the last number of years in San Diego has landed the very next week. When I was in Northern California, it often fell on the actual week of our anniversary and we would just get away after camp to celebrate. But because the "actual date" of our anniversary was now open for the first time in a long time, we tried to celebrate it on the right day. Novel idea, I know. But to pull this off, I would have to work hard to get everything done before we left and got away. I tried, but it wasn't working. Someone inevitably called for a last-minute detail, and I pulled away from our anniversary weekend to respond. Some detail didn't get done, and then my computer ended up coming with us on our date weekend so I could do work. I'm trying desperately to move the fulcrum of my life to directly under the weight of my marriage, but the pressure on the work side is just too great that week.

Last year, I extensively warned everyone from every church at this summer camp I run that I would be unreachable during this week—but the same thing still happened. So Shannon and

I looked at each other and said, "Who are we kidding? This isn't working. Something has to give." So in our context, this year we moved our anniversary celebration up two weeks. Now Shannon and I will be retreating in early June instead of two days before summer camp. The fulcrum will move to marriage for three days, and then in the 10 days of camp and preparation, it will move the other direction.

You can get mad and say that's not balance, but that's not reality either. For us, even though the search can drive us crazy, finding the fulcrum movement is the only way we can create even the semblance of balance. I don't think we can ditch the need for balance, but I also think we must redefine it or it will never happen.

So how's your balance? How mobile is your fulcrum? What seasons of life naturally put pressure on the balance myth in your marriage, and how can you move the fulcrum intentionally to even relax the stress of life?

CHAPTER SIXTEEN

SOMETIMES my wife texts me to say, "I like you." What can I say? She's a good love-note texter. She chooses those words because she knows that the phrase "I love you," however powerful and intentional it may be, can represent an obligation more than a desire. Yes, we love one another and often say so. But I'm called by Jesus to love even my enemies. It doesn't mean I'm going to like them. So when my wife or I tell each other, "I like you," it sometimes carries more weight.

There's something sweet about adoption in this regard, too. It's a choice, and when you choose someone, it's soul-nourishing. It's the beauty and power of Romans 5:8—*But God demonstrates his own love for us in this: While we were still sinners, Christ died for us.* It's the affirmation of Paul when he wrote this: *For he chose us in him before the creation of the world to be holy and blameless in his sight (Ephesians 1:4).* We are a chosen people, and that is an epic part of God's story and a powerful image in marriage.

In the case of our marriage, there are other really powerful phrases, too—especially in light of the love language discussion when I discovered that my wife values "words of affirmation."

- I cherish you.

- I need you.

- I want to be with you.

- You're it in my world.

Those are all invaluable phrases in our marriage. But still, the one that means more than almost anything else is this one: "I'm with you." It means that no matter what you decide or how it actually turns out, I've got your back. I'm with you. The problem is that everything around us seems to want to push us out of the "I'm with you" mindset.

Our kids have a way of trying to divide us. They'll ask one of us something and then go to the other and ask the same thing. When they get caught in this, the consequence for them is severe. But they still try from time to time to divide us.

Even the categories for this book feature a division of sorts. Take care of you. Then take care of your marriage. Then take care of your family. Then take care of your ministry. Seems like each then has its own pull and its own category. They have that myth of balance to them somewhere. They seem to demand that when I give time or energy to one of them, I'm taking it from another. When this is how it feels, then no matter how you seek balance or how you spread your time, your spouse will always feel like they are not getting enough of you.

The truth is, compartmentalization of life is draining, and it's false. Life doesn't have stay in nice little boxes like that; instead, every area flows over into every other area. I don't have a social life, a work life, a personal life, a sex life, and a family life. I just have a life, and every single one of my decisions affects every other area of me. In marriage, we can add another level of complexity because the biblical truth is the "two are now one" (see Matthew 19:5-6). So while my wife and I remain individuals, we also are an inseparable unit, and everything we do or say affects the other. Not being "with you" is not really an option. But a spiritual truth does not predetermine a practical reality. We have to work at this constantly.

I have to be "with my wife" more than just when I'm physically with her. No, not that I can teleport myself or that I'm advocating a "with you in spirit" idea. "I'm with you" means that when my wife goes to work as a substitute teacher and I go to the church as a youth pastor, we have not gone our separate ways. We actually have sent each other to do the thing we agree is important. We don't divide and conquer. We unite and accomplish. We are one couple doing separate things.

I know that sounds subtle and perhaps paradoxical, but I think it is critical to wrap our heads around this truth in marriage. It's not my wife's job to raise the kids and my job to raise the money. It's our job to do both, and at times, we agree to send one another off to do one part of that collective priority. But an "us" reality is not natural. We live in an individualistic culture, and operating as a team and choosing to mourn, laugh, work, and play in support of each other is an uphill battle.

Patrick Lencioni examines this extensively in the leadership parable he wrote for marriages and families titled *The Three Big Questions for a Frantic Family*, and it's well worth your read. It's all about how to apply goal setting and priorities in the ebb and flow of real family life. Like most of his books, it's written in a novel/parable form. The bottom line of the book is that every marriage and every family should be able to define its "rally cry" for the next three months. What is the thing that we as a couple need to say, "I'm with you in this"? If you're in the middle of having a baby, then this will be easy. If you're purchasing a house or trying to get out of credit card debt, or if one of you is trying to finish a graduate degree, then you'll be able to identify this with very little work. The "rally cry" is clear, and the steps necessary to stack hands on this "I'm with you" statement are almost self-evident.

But in the "normal" rhythms of life, it is a little harder. (Lencioni has some great free downloadable worksheets on his website[4] if you want to dive into this, too.) It requires that we communicate with each other what we fear, hope, and dream about. We must have conversations about what really needs to happen and what it will take for us to pull this off, even if one of us will shoulder the weight of the task. It means we carry the weight of our life together and move money, time, and support toward that common goal. It is a very intentional "I'm with you" in this pull.

Go ahead. Tell your spouse "I love you" and "I like you," and then sit down and decide what that really means. Where are the places "I'm with you," and where are the "I'm not with you" points that deserve some attention? Figuring this out will affect everything, and to that end, "I'm with you" in this goal for our marriages.

SECTION THREE

THE BEST GIFT I CAN GIVE MY COMMUNITY AND MINISTRY IS A HEALTHY FAMILY

I've never been to Australia. My grandma went there when I was in high school and brought me back a boomerang. My sister-in-law lived there for a year after college graduation and did the same. The couple that are the primary fundraisers and directors of the orphanage that Becky and Billy were adopted from are Australian, not Ugandan. A key volunteer in my current ministry grew up there, has family there, and visits once a year. I've seen movies and pictures, and I've read articles about it. So I think I know some stuff about Australia.

But because I've never seen it firsthand, I'm sure that I have some stuff wrong. I think all the oceans that surround it are all beautiful and blue. I think everyone drives a four-wheel drive, off-road vehicle. I think the only toys kids play with are boomerangs. Like Texas, they evidently pride themselves on things being oversized. On a globe, it feels like I could drive just about anywhere in a day. But the only real taste I get of Australia is through the lens of others around me and their experiences. Based on what they say and do, I decide whether or not I would want to go visit for myself. All of my assumptions and understanding about Australia have been acquired this way.

In our American culture, this is largely how many people experience the Christian faith as well. They don't do it firsthand, they only have secondhand observations, and they make assumptions and come to conclusions about God and Jesus based on those observations. "Wait," you say. "Some people I know who are far from God have experienced it firsthand, too." Yup, and what they tasted was so distasteful that they spit it out.

And if that is true of faith, it is even truer of a healthy Christian family.

What does "healthy Christian family" even mean anymore? I have one student in my small group whose parents are divorced, and when he's at his mom's house, he can't sleep in a bedroom because there are six cats in there and the entire room is their litter box. He's 17 and thinks it's normal. I have another young woman in our ministry whose mom has been divorced and remarried four times, and she calls each of the men "Dad." To add more fuel to the fire, her mom's current husband is the best friend of husband No. 3. And get this, husband No. 3 is on disability and lives downstairs while husband No. 4 and mom live upstairs. It gets crazier if I keep going, but I won't.

Needless to say, a "normal" two-parent home with a few kids and a car in the driveway is not normal. I'm not sure it ever was normal, but it definitely hasn't been around for a long time if it was. In fact, what is normal for our world today (including the inner city, my suburban world, and even our rural communities), quite honestly, is tragic. But tragic is so normal that people don't even see it as abnormal anymore.

Wanna change your world? Wanna give your ministry and your local community a taste of the radical faith of Jesus? Then give your marriage a healthy you. Give your kids a healthy marriage. And please give your community a healthy family. It might be the only chance they have ever had to experience it.

CHAPTER SEVENTEEN

NO, IT'S NOT MULTIPLICATION; IT'S DIVISION

HI, my name is Brian and I'm a field-trip dad. That's right. I've been to the zoo so many times I can walk it blindfolded. I know where the local aquarium and nature preserves are. I know how to make a sack lunch that can be fully thrown away. I am the master at sitting on a yellow school bus and knowing to be quiet when the teacher holds up a hand and nonverbally begins the five-finger countdown. I can even give you the bus safety speech in case the driver is voiceless on my next trip. I have lots of pictures of me with my kids visiting tide pools and touching weird things. I also have been tragically scarred by moms in low-rise jeans who tie kids' shoes and show the world their rump. I laugh with my wife and tell her about what I now call the "mom thong" sighting. Plumbers ain't got nothing on field-trip moms.

But anyway, I remember sitting with my oldest son, T.J., on a trip home from the tide pools in fourth grade and asking him, "How did you like it?" I expected him to say something about the animals we saw or the sandcastle he made, but instead he said, "Thanks for coming, Dad. I really like having you at field trips. Thanks for spending time with me." That was nice, but that's not why I remember it. I remember it because of what he said next: "Oh, and thanks for not pulling out your phone." I was shocked. I had put it on silent and chose to ignore it, but I had no idea T.J. would notice, and he hadn't complained about it before. But this said at least two things: (1) I'm on my phone more than I notice, and (2) my kids are watching.

As I thought about this, it was a clear reminder to me that my kids are not just watching tide pool animals, they're also watching everything and learning lots by accidental observation. They're learning about marriage by how I talk to and treat their mom. They're learning about work, church, love, faith, risk—even lawn mowing and car driving. Seriously, they're learning all of it by observation, and often when I least think about it, they are watching. I remember driving Tyler home from an after-school run to grab a smoothie one time, and he asked me, "Why do you take your foot off the gas when you shift the car gears?" I thought, "Oh man, I'm in trouble." These five sets of young eyes in my house are observing my every move and expecting my life to be mimic-worthy. I'd better get my head in the game and keep it there.

In the fall of 2009, while at the National Youth Workers Convention in Los Angeles, I heard a talk by Shane Hipps that rocked my world. He was talking about technology and said all of it can be a tool for life and ministry, but it also all comes with a price tag. He talked about grief as an example. He reminded us that when life gets really tough, people don't need our words. They just need us to be there for them. He mentioned how technology can only take us relationally so far in this. It is impossible for you to "just be present" with a grieving family by calling them. You can't have them leave you on speaker on the table while you sit quietly to be present in their mourning. That's ludicrous. In the same way, I can't give my son an iPhone®, have him turn it on while I turn mine on so he can let me watch the game using FaceTime®, and then say, "Thanks for letting me come to your soccer game." I can only attend the game in the flesh.

As if that wasn't enough of a reminder, Hipps then said this kicker: "There is no such thing as multitasking. It doesn't multiply anything; it only divides." I wanted to stand up and say, "What are you talking about? I can watch TV and fold laundry. My wife says she can watch TV, fold laundry, help with homework, check out Facebook, and take the dog for a walk. Multitasking is totally possible." But to prove his point, he suggested that we consider our daily lives to be a glass of water. He said that if you take a glass of water and pour it into four glasses, you don't generate any new water—you just divide up the water you had. The same is true of multitasking. You don't actually generate any new work or multiply energy; you just divide up your attention and lessen your influence.

He blew a hole in so many myths I had as a parent. He was right: I can't be present in more than one place at a time, and technology doesn't change that. I can't fully do two things at once. All I can do is decide that some task is not worth all my attention. For example, I can drive and listen to music, but only when neither requires my undivided attention. If I come up on a car crash or if the fog drops visibility down to 20 feet in front of me, I'll slow down and turn off the radio. Driving suddenly gets all of me.

This really messed with me. This means that if I want to be fully present with my kids, I have to be fully present. Just yesterday I was working on this book at home and forgot it was a short day at school. I had the house to myself and was crankin' away when three of my kids came home and wanted to tell me all about their day. I tried to both give them an ear and stay in my train of thought as I typed. But my wife was watching the ridiculousness of this attempt and said, "Brian, you're going to have to put down the computer and talk to your kids for a few. Then you can go work somewhere else." She was right. I still try to multitask, but it's impossible. For this same reason, Shannon and I have tried to make a pact to turn off our cell phones and put down computers from the time I get home from work until the kids' 8:30 p.m. bedtime. When we hold this as sacred (and some days we fail) we're more invested and attentive to our family. Our conversations are better. Our impact is greater. Our lives are fuller.

For me this also means:

- I can't watch my kid's game and answer the phone.

- I can't surf the Internet and chat on Facebook and talk to my mom on the phone.

- I can't text someone else while listening to the conversation or meeting I'm in.

It also means that I must keep reminding myself that if I really want my life to matter, then I need to fully devote myself to what I'm doing at that moment. And the more important the task, the truer this becomes. If I'm preparing a sermon, I need to do that. If I'm driving my family on vacation, I need to do that. If I'm reading a book with my kids, I need to do that. My impact will be greater if I just do one thing—fully. And if the subject is parenting, then really, is there a more important task?

Maybe we need to put a death bullet in the heart of the multitasking lie and just be present—*especially* with our kids. We can't multiply ourselves. All we can do is divide.

CHAPTER EIGHTEEN

DITCH THE BUNKER-AND THE HELICOPTER, TOO

"**IF** it ain't broke, don't fix it." That's why I haven't fixed the sink in our kitchen. Don't get me wrong—it is chipped, outdated, stained a weird shade of yellowish brown that full-strength bleach can't dent, and in need of replacement, but it still holds water and therefore works! But I promise you that if I "fix it," 12 other things will move from "ain't broke" to "broke" in the process, and it will be a nightmare. So until I'm ready for a full kitchen remodel, "the ain't broke" sink won't get fixed. The truth is, I'm actually praying that my upstairs master bathroom floods in some miracle of God and completely ruins both my bathroom and the kitchen below. That would make a HUGE mess, but it would be awesome because they are both nasty and insurance would kick in to fix them.

But I digress. My point is that while my sink may have problems but won't get fixed, this is not true of everything we might put in the "ain't broke" category. There are some things in life that seem to be working just fine that we need to declare broken. I could give you a long list of other plumbing things that fall under this category in my life—like the leaking water main in my front yard. But this is not a plumbing nightmare chapter; it's a family one and some "Christian" parenting falls under this category for me. This chapter might get me in some hot water, but here it goes.

When our kids were young—around preschool age—we told them very clearly that their job was to "listen and obey" and that our job was to "provide and protect." If you asked them, they could repeat it back to you like little robots. We did this because it was not my kid's job to fully understand what a burn was or why they couldn't play in the street. At a certain age, they just needed to obey first and ask questions second. In that regard, all the onus of responsibility and safety lay on us as parents. If they just did what they were told, then it was our job to make sure they couldn't do anything that would cause them undue harm.

For example, when Tyler was 11 months old we left him and his older brother with some friends while we went out to dinner. While Tyler was wandering around the house like a newly mobile child does, he got too close to the wood stove and reached out to grab it to stabilize himself. The result was a second-degree burn on his little paw that left him in a month-long state of gauze pad. He was so young and his skin so forgivable that today he doesn't even have a scar to show for it. But our friends felt horrible because they knew it was not Tyler's fault. It was their job to protect, not Tyler's.

When we first moved to San Diego, it was our turn. Not with burns or Tyler, but with our 3-year-old Jake and the beach. Once we took our family to a busy Coronado beach with some friends. Everything was going fine, and I was playing with four kids making a sandcastle. Shannon and I each thought the other parent had Jake. That is, until we heard the lifeguard vehicle P.A. announce, "We have a blond boy named Jake. He says he's 3. If this is your son, please come get him." We were mortified. Jake thought it was awesome because he got to ride in a cool Jeep, hear his name said over that loudspeaker thing, and meet the lifeguards. We didn't even know he was gone. But again, it was not Jake's fault that he did what 3-year-olds do. It was ours for not knowing where he was. Thankfully both of those stories have a happy ending, but not all parenting mistakes end so painlessly.

At some point we have to realize that this parenting plan has an expiration date. At a certain age, and not much beyond kindergarten, my wife and I are no longer the only ones responsible for the provision or protection of my kid's life. And it's not because they now have teachers that are responsible for them when I'm not looking. The truth is that our kids have to start taking some responsibility for their own lives. For example, when I teach them to ride a bike, they are also old enough to know why they have to wear a helmet or why they can't ride in a busy street. Sure, if I see them fail to do this, there are repercussions for them. But I'm not the only one responsible for their protection. They must begin to take part in this role, too.

No, my job doesn't stop being "provide and protect," but it does morph into "teach my kids to provide and protect for themselves." For whatever reason, some parents never make the morph. I'm not kidding you. They see their job as being the sole protector of their kids, and they have reduced parenting to a strictly defensive posture. It's popularly called two things: bunker parenting and helicopter parenting. I think it's time to declare these ideas officially "broke" and ditch the bunker mindset and the helicopter parenting. Both are shortsighted, don't work, and are rooted in paranoia.

Bunker parenting means our parenting role is primarily to "wall off" evil. As long as our kids are safe in my protective bunker, things will be just fine. By the time these kids make it to high school, their innocence has moved to ignorance, and they are prime targets for the enemy.

When my wife and I moved to San Diego, we got zoo passes. We took our kids all the time, and as a result I found out that there was a really nice restaurant hidden inside. So one summer night for a date, I took Shannon to the zoo for dinner. I know; I'm the man. Don't act like you're not jealous. Anyway, after dinner, we went for a walk and saw the zoo at dusk. Seriously, it was the zoo like I'd never seen it before. One place we walked through is called "Cat Canyon," home to the panthers, snow leopards, and tigers. When you go in the middle of a hot day on a field trip with a school or your family, they are all literally taking a catnap in their dens and you rarely see them. It's boring and all you see is empty cages with pictures and labels of what is supposed to be in there. But at dusk they were all up and active, and because I had just finished watching Planet Earth, I knew that the snow leopard was extremely rare and had been filmed hunting in the wild just once. So when I saw two of them walking around, I was just mesmerized and stood forever watching their big fluffy tails go back and forth in the cage.

But then I remembered that these snow leopards were not "real" snow leopards anymore. Sure, they walk like it and look like it, but if you take them and release them into the wild, they will die because they have lost the ability to survive outside of captivity.

This is the problem with bunker parenting. Yes, it keeps kids safe, but only as long as you have them in the cage. This is why they can't go out with friends. This is why they're not allowed to use the Internet unfiltered. It is why they live in the land where parents are the monarchy of the home space. We say it keeps them safe. The reality is that when this is our primary parenting model, it just raises spoon-fed tigers, not real animals capable of survival in the wild—and you and I both know it's a jungle out there. Bunker parenting is not the solution.

Helicopter parenting is the airborne version of bunker parenting. The parents are not shepherds of their kids; they are private investigators stalking them. In the worst cases, by the time their children get to high school, these parents actually track kids with GPS units in their cars and software on their cell phones. I'm not saying these things never have their place or that some trust can't be destroyed so badly that it's warranted. But I am saying this is not the goal. Getting a child to behave when I'm the cop in the rearview mirror watching their every move is not training a child; it's manipulating. No one really wants to track their kids like this for the rest of their lives.

The bigger problem is that the issue is often not really the child in the first place. The reason they can't go to the dance or to the youth group mission trip or to the neighbors to spend the night is not because of a child issue—it's because of a parent issue. The parents simply blame the child for their own inability to trust anyone. In helicopter parenting, their "provide and protect" mindset has gone from a healthy responsibility to a paranoid obsession. The truth is, my role as a parent is not to follow my child around, checking on everything the teacher might have said, or to run ahead, clearing the path of all possible danger. I cannot ensure my child will never see, hear, or come into contact with evil. That's an impossible task. Instead we need to train our kids how to respond on their own when evil does show up.

Helicopter parenting sounds good, like parents are doing their job and have not abdicated their role. But down deep, if we're honest, this is rooted in a failure to trust God. Helicopter parents don't believe God can protect or even that they can train a child to defend without them and won't own up to their own fears. The result is a child who never grows up, staying a child without discernment because they are never given the freedom to fail.

So here's one idea at a solution. It's not comprehensive, but it is a start in a different direction. I have this phrase I use with our youth ministry volunteers that influences and informs my own parenting toward this end: "Give them enough rope to trip on, but not enough to hang themselves with." Let me explain. For my own kids and the students I work with, the older and more responsible they become, the more rope I give them. When T.J. was turning 6, his grandma brought him a bike jump to our camping trip for his birthday. It was about 6 feet long and about a foot off the ground when fully assembled. It had a ramp up, a table-like thing in the middle, and then a ramp down.

To his young adventure-filled eyes, it was the greatest thing ever. To his mom and I, we knew it represented blood, bruises, falls, and maybe even trips to the hospital. So I walked up to T.J., strapped his helmet on, and said, "You can ride this, just so long as you know you're going to get hurt." The look on his face was priceless. You'd have thought I'd just told him it was going to explode and send shrapnel and body parts flying everywhere when he went on it. He had not for a moment processed that this was an option. He said, "Going to get hurt?" I said, "Yes, you will get hurt. It will be fun, and eventually, you'll fall less. But especially as you learn, you're going to get hurt. When you fall, it will likely scrape something up and there might be blood, too. If you don't want to risk that, then don't go off the jump."

I could see T.J.'s brain turning as he weighed his options. Keep my jump but maybe get hurt. Lose my jump but stay safer. Then he concluded, "OK, Dad. If I get hurt, we'll just wash it off and I'll go again." Off he went. And I didn't set the jump up next to a cliff or in the street filled with speeding cars. In other words, "He had enough rope to trip on, but not enough to hang himself."

Now he's a freshman and heads off to dances I can't chaperone and to places I can't secure. Soon he'll drive a car I can't control—and asking "How much rope is too much?" is not so easy. But bunkering him down or flying a helicopter over his life are not solutions either. If we want to raise capable and confident adults who grow to make right choices on their own, then we have to give our children the freedom to fail. Failure to do this will only perpetuate their childhood, not move them out of it.

CHAPTER NINETEEN

FORMULA SCHMORMULA

MAYBE the most misused verse in the Bible is this one: *Train up a child in the way he should go, Even when he is old he will not depart from it (Proverbs 22:6 NASB)*. I once took a seminary class on the books of the Bible and how to rightly interpret them, and the professor made us all repeat this mantra over and over again: "Proverbs are not promises." I hate that. I really wish they were. Then I'd know how to get rich, how to be happy, and how to raise my kids perfectly. But someone needs to share this truth with the people who make those posters and plaques they sell in bookstores next to the Testamints® and Thomas Kinkade cups. The wisdom literature in the Bible has general truth in it, but it is not prophecy.

When it comes to parenting, there is no formula, and you can't manufacture a Jesus-following child, no matter how strong your efforts or how flawless your training. My call for us to stop bunker and helicopter parenting is not a promise of future success based on a new model. It is simply a broken system we can't place our trust in, like some kind of formula for parenting in a dangerous world. This is brutal, but nonetheless true.

I can think of families that did some things I would never do and ended up with children who passionately follow Jesus. One of those former students literally just hit a button on Facebook "liking Jesus' Facebook page" as I typed this. Yes, evidently Jesus has a Facebook page. Now you know; you can thank me later. Anyway, like any good, easily distracted youth pastor, I paused this writing to that diversion and wrote on his wall: "Just saw you like Jesus. Good job. Hope all is well." He commented back to me, "I love Jesus and I'm trying to give him more of me every day. Thank you, Brian, for being my youth pastor. God got ahold of me, I'm going to be a missionary, and now I'm working in a life-changing ministry for trouble teenagers. I just finished up one-and-a-half years of Bible college and am planning on finishing. God is so good." If you knew his whole story, this would seem ridiculous to you; it did not follow the formula.

I can think of lots of families with parents that didn't go to church, didn't love God, and didn't raise kids even close to the way they should go—but whose kids now love and serve God with their lives. Your own life or maybe even your pastor might have that very story. It's not my story, but it is the story of my lead pastor at our church. I grew up going to church; he didn't step foot into one until he was 15. Just yesterday I cried and prayed with a young woman in our ministry whose mom tells her that she was a mistake and wishes she was never born. If you applied the parenting formula to this teenager's life, then she should never follow God a day in her life. But she was in tears asking me how she can honor and serve God when her family is falling apart and saying these horrible lies. It doesn't mean her mom is not passing on horrible negative consequences that are greatly shaping her daughter, but it does mean that evidently the Proverbs 22:6 parenting formula is not the defining factor in her life. I guess I can chalk those stories up to grace trumping the formula, and I can even praise God for them.

But that's not so easy for the families that seemed to follow the formula. What do you do with the families who, for all practical purposes, aced the test but whose children have gone in different directions, making tragic choices? They did everything "by the book" and seemed to pay the price, shedding tears and asking God, "Why?" I've cried with them. I've counseled them. I've scratched my head in wonder. I've watched as they have gone to great lengths to love and lead their children, only to have the process fall apart.

I want to flip a table and say, "That's not right." It shouldn't work like this. I'm not talking about pastors who loved the church more than they loved their family. It's not families who loved soccer more than they loved Jesus. These are highly involved, grace-filled, loving people whose children said no to Jesus despite their upbringing. I wish so badly that I could point to the thing they did wrong. I want to believe that if I could unpack their parenting and hear the whole story, I could find the problem and fix it. But it's not there. There is no silver bullet.

So what do you do with that? How do we let this truth inform our parenting without crippling it? Like a conversation about the doctrine of predestination, it's easy to just throw up our hands and decide that nothing matters and quit trying. But clearly, the stakes are too high for us to bail. We can't give up, but we can quit trusting the wrong things. We can let this drive us to our knees in prayer, asking God to lead our children in places that our good Christian formulas cannot. We can beg God to protect and do the miraculous, and we can trust that God loves our children more than we do. We also can quit searching for the "one wrong thing" we're doing or the magic pill that will make everything right.

I still remember vividly the day that a Kirby® vacuum salesman came to our front door. I was in high school, and this young man in his 20s showed up at our door to ask us if we needed a new vacuum. We had this old puke green noisy thing that puffed and fumed when the bag was full, so the answer clearly was "yes." So we invited the vacuum wizard into our home, and he proceeded to give us the display of a lifetime. He spread stuff on our carpet and then tried to suck it up with our dead beast. Then afterward he went over it with his vacuum and emptied the bag to show us all the stuff our death trap had left behind. He told us that we were breathing bad things and that his vacuum could deliver better health, peace of mind, and the clean house my mom desired to provide for her family.

We were sold. My mom wanted it, and my sister and I thought it was the greatest invention since the automobile, but my dad was not having it. The vacuum cost more than our house payment, and he agreed that this demonstration proved we needed a new vacuum. But he said we could go on vacation for what this one was going to cost and we'd buy a different one instead. The man rallied us all again and told my dad that even a new vacuum would not do the trick, giving compelling arguments and virtually offering free steak knives just to sweeten the offer. He said aerospace engineers had designed this vacuum, and we believed it was like Jesus in an appliance.

Again we begged my dad to sign our lives away for this contract, and finally, after more than an hour of demonstrations and sales pitching, my dad got angry and chased this salesman out of our house, telling him to never come back again. My dad was mad—and right. The vacuum was overpriced and surely would have under-delivered.

It's time that we as parents realize parenting is a lot like cleaning a house. You can't hire a robot to do it or buy some gadget that makes it instantly happen or guarantee things will never get dirty again. You don't need a new formula or vacuum or some magic paste they sell at the county fair. Clean homes and God-honoring families happen slowly, with some days better than others. Houses that are actually lived in get dirty, and no one's parenting holds the secret ingredient. If there is a formula, 18 years of youth ministry and 14 years of parenting haven't revealed it to me, and if I had it, this book would be a way bigger seller than it surely will be.

So from one parent to another, just hang in there. Don't quit. Don't trust the lies. We need you. Your kids need you. The kingdom of God needs you. One day at a time, one decision at a time, one failure and one success at a time, keep at it. Lean on God. Lean on grace. Beg God in prayer, and know this: You're in a wide stream of God-fearing, Jesus-following parents deep in the thick of it with you, all desperately asking the Holy Spirit to lead us each step of this crazy way.

CHAPTER TWENTY

THE POWER OF YOU

AS I mentioned earlier, every fall I take our high school men to the desert for a man trip weekend. Think stereotypical redneck man stuff. We drive out in four-wheel drive vehicles, refuse to shower or shave, pack way too much meat and potatoes, transport a ridiculous amount of guns and ammo, have the biggest bonfire you've ever seen, and basically blow all kinds of things up. We're in the middle of absolute nowhere on Bureau of Land Management space, surrounded by sand, rock mountains, and essentially zero vegetation. You couldn't set the place on fire if you poured gasoline on it and lit it. OK, so we might have tried that, too. Trust me, nothing burns out there.

In our attempt to outdo ourselves and to trump the previous year's explosion, last year we discovered the beauty of this stuff called Tannerite. It's totally legal and not explosive—that is, until you mix it together with an activator and then shoot it with a high-powered rifle round. Then it's very explosive. If you mix some of it up, attach it to a five-gallon propane tank, start a fire around it, and then shoot it from 200 yards away, then what you have is a very explosive "don't tell your mom about this" kind of moment.

It's awesome and powerful. So powerful that it makes for a perfect illustration to talk to teenage guys about the power of their decisions in shaping their lives. We talk to them about their sexuality, their words, their actions, and their motives. We challenge them to live dangerously for God. We challenge them to take wise risks and blow stuff up from 200 yards away. And we don't wince away or tell them to calm down. They are powerful men, and if their lives are set clearly on the tracks of faith in Jesus, they can and should be a strong force for the kingdom of God. Oh, how I yearn for that in the young men I'm raising up.

In the same way, if I could be so bold, can I remind you that you are a powerful force? You are Tannerite-explosion powerful and dangerous for the kingdom of God. You are more powerful than any influence in your child's life. You are more powerful than teachers at school, friends, Hollywood, or music. In fact, the greatest shot your kid has at becoming a Jesus-following young man or woman as an adult is your influence on their childhood.

No, it's not a formula, but it is a reality, and you are called by God to leverage it. I don't need a child development study or statistic to verify it. I know it. You know it. Just talk to anyone about their story, and for better or worse, they'll start somewhere in their childhood. It's where we all begin physically, spiritually, emotionally, mentally, and every other kind of "-ally"—under the direct influence of our guardians.

There's no way around it: Childhood critically shapes each person's story, and the role of a parent in that environment is beyond comparison. Regardless of socioeconomic status, race, career, or even religious beliefs, every parent on the planet is deeply shaping the lives of their children, and as youth workers, we're certainly no exception to the rule. We are all explosive and powerful influences on the lives of our children, and it's time to strap on the ear and eye protection, clear the area, and strike the match. We have no time to lose.

If I could wave a magic wand over the world and get parents to do just one thing that many have mental agreement with but very little real action behind, I'd tell them to leverage their influence and have consistent one-on-one time with their kids. Like a desert explosion, there's no greater way I know of to gain the influence and attention of your child than this. When I ask or challenge families to let me take their sons to the desert, moms worry and dads grunt and ask if they can come, to which we say, "It's OK, Mom—and we leave at 3 p.m., Dad." When I ask those same parents to leverage their influence and have a one-on-one mentoring relationship with their son, most just look at me and nod their heads and smile.

I didn't ask them to do something that sounded ridiculous, like send their kid to an explosion retreat, but it's also not likely to happen. If questioned, they will tell me that they have too many children, too full a life, and that they do other things with their kids. I'm convinced it would help most, if not all families— even ones where parents aren't followers of Christ—if they did this with their kids. If I were given only one weapon in my arsenal on how to help Christian families to raise a child into a young adult who loves Jesus, I'd simply ask parents to spend intentional one-on-one time with their kids. Period.

In the famous words of G.I. Joe®, "Now you know, and knowing is half the battle"—but it IS only half the battle! (I really wish I had a reason to throw in a ThunderCats® cartoon quote here, too. But "ThunderCats, ThunderCats, ThunderCats, Hoooo!" has zero meaning for anything except '80s bonding with a small percentage of you. Thanks for entertaining me.) The truth is we all know stuff that we don't do anything with. I know that flossing makes my dentist happy, and she tells me it will save me money and give me fewer cavities. Despite the fact that both results sound good to me, knowing this doesn't mean I floss after every meal or that I won't be mad when I have to pay for another cavity filling.

I also know that driving the speed limit on tires with the correct air pressure while easing into and out of the gas pedal will increase my fuel mileage considerably as I drive. This, too, will save me money. But that doesn't mean I drive slower or pull away from a stop with greater patience. It just means I know stuff.

While I'm guessing there might be some parents out there who will claim that their influence on their child is not more powerful than that of some peer group, it would not be hard to statistically demonstrate[5] that while their kids' peers might have influence, a fully engaged parent is proven to win the battle time and time again. But that is only knowledge, and the distance between head and hand can sometimes be miles apart. Convincing someone of a truth and moving that person to action as a result of that truth are as different as night and day. In a lot of ways, it's why I could make an argument against the effectiveness of the proclamational preaching model. It's not that it's bad to motivate someone verbally; it's just that cognitive agreement unaccompanied by authentic life change is merely lip service and wishful thinking. It's the age-old faith-and-deeds argument. *But someone will say, "You have faith; I have deeds." Show me your faith without deeds, and I will show you my faith by my deeds (James 2:18).*

I'm not trying to discredit the influence a parent can have through other forms of involvement, or the role of small groups or the church or any other influential relationship in the life of a child. But I am saying that you are POWERFUL and that it's time to leverage it for everything you've got. While there is no shortcut to influence, there is a clear relationship between time spent and influence had. The more time you spend with your child, the more influence you'll have on your child.

It's also important to remember that kids are different in a one-on-one setting. All kids are. I know they are essentially the same in personality and such, but stuff comes out in one-on-

one conversations that simply won't be seen or heard or found anywhere else. If we don't go to the desert, we can't blow stuff up. In the same way, certain conversations simply need a safer place to happen, and these spaces provide just that.

And if that's not enough to move you, can I remind you that the patterns you're setting at a young age are the ones you'll be leaning on in their critical teen years when relationships between children and parents are typically the most strained? The truth is, in almost two decades of youth ministry, I've never had a counseling appointment with a parent about their teenager where the parent was doing this. Whenever I ask, "Do you and your son or daughter have a regular, standing lunch date or java chat or Saturday breakfast or anything that is consistent and just the two of you?" the answer is always "No." Doing so isn't some miracle fix to all parenting problems, but it solves a myriad of communication issues.

As an example, here's how this works in my house. It's not going to sound very explosive, but I believe it is powerful. For our family, about the time that I can start having real conversations with my kids and their brains start moving toward critical thinking skills, I begin weekly one-on-one chats. With my oldest son, I didn't start until he was in sixth grade. In my mind, I thought it would be a middle school tradition with my kids— kind of like a rite of passage. Because our local middle school starts school an hour later than the elementary school, I figured I could just ease into this, adding them one at a time as they hit sixth grade, taking them to breakfast to chat and then to school.

But as I've quickly seen the benefit of it, I've dropped the threshold down to fourth grade and currently meet weekly with three of my kids: one in fourth grade, one in sixth, and one in ninth. Before that, it was a car ride here and there with just me on our way home from church. It's a Christmas daddy date with my daughter. It's a trip to the hardware store and a "Shhh, don't tell mom" trip to get ice cream with one of them. These one-on-one chats are hit-and-miss until fourth grade for our family. But then things change.

Currently, on Monday afternoon after school, I get a hazelnut Americano. My 9-year-old son, Jake, gets an ice cream sandwich. On Wednesday morning I get a hazelnut Americano. My 14-year-old son, T.J., gets a Gatorade® and a bagel with ham and cheese. On Thursday morning I get a hazelnut Americano. My 12-year-old son, Tyler, gets a blended vanilla chai and a bagel with ham and cheese. It's all at the same coffee shop around the corner from our house. The owner, Joe, now knows us by name, has at least my order memorized, and brings it to our table in this local java spot. We exchange wisecracks and complain about the service. He misses us when we're not there. It's the same every week. Yes, it's monotonous, but yes, it's paying off.

Don't get me wrong; not every conversation is life-altering. Sometimes we read some article or watch a video on my iPhone to get the conversation going, something that afterward I can say, "So, what do you think about that?" Sometimes it's just silly and we laugh about nothing, playing "would you rather" games and wondering if you'd rather eat boogers for dinner or sleep in a giant bowl of spaghetti.

But over time, I'm building relationships with my kids. And over time, little by little, they're confiding in me their emotions, fears, dreams, and even some questions they've been wondering about. Slowly and methodically, the monotony is deepening our relationship and transforming us. Yes, they have others they talk to, and no, I'm not the only person on the planet they can confide in. But it's not just breakfast either. It is earning the right to be heard and it's consistent enough that when issues come up, it's also not an "OK, what did I do this time?" meeting with Dad either.

I don't know how you are consciously leveraging your powerful influence as a parent. We are all leveraging it in some capacity. The only question at this point is, "How?" If I could leverage any influence I've gained as you read this book, I'd beg you to please invest in one-on-one connection points with your kids. It might take years to see the results, but slowly and methodically, you'll literally change their lives, your life, and the world around you if you do. You are powerful. Light the fuse and pull the trigger.

CHAPTER TWENTY-ONE

MAKIN' MEMORIES THAT LAST

AS a kid, I grew up camping in the redwoods of Northern California every summer for two weeks with my cousins. My mom and my grandma would take my sister and I and my four cousins somewhere for a week in one campground and then we'd move to another campground and my dad would meet us for the second week. We rode bikes, we fished, we got in trouble. We played Hide-and-Seek and Capture the Flag in canyons and creek beds. We went on hikes and got lost, pooped in the woods, jumped off stuff, and got into stuff. We even once had a huge apple fight, flinging dead fruit with sticks at each other in an orchard along the river at Albee Creek.

I remember peeing in fires once with Uncle Spud. Yes, I had an Uncle Spud, and yes, peeing in fires creates a horrible smell. I remember the countless tiny trout we caught that my grandma and my mom fried for breakfast, and the pies my grandma baked in her trailer. I remember our two trips to Hawaii, road trips with my dad fishing, and various backpacking trips. They all are stuck in my brain even long after my grandma and the photographs have faded.

This is somewhat amazing because when it comes to memories, I'm a forgetter. It's my Achilles' heel in ministry and life. I'm constantly forgetting names, things I've done, and lessons I've taught. I forget all kinds of stuff. When it comes to forgiving people, this makes life super easy, because half the time I don't even remember what they did that they think I should still be upset about. It also means I let the same people hurt me the same way all the time because I forgot what they did the last time. Most of the time, I'm not a fan of my forgetfulness.

If your brain is a memory machine, I confess that I'm jealous. I'm constantly praying that God would show me some power food that I should eat to make my brain work better, or that God would just miraculously give me a photographic memory so that I could recall stuff on a whim. I would give big money for a duct tape brain. But despite my amazing ability to forget stuff, I have miraculously held on to, across the board, my childhood memories tied to vacationing. It's like they hold some kind of memory glue that other information simply does not have.

I'm sure your family dinners are making memories for you and your kids. Go ahead and keep making them a priority. Your kids will thank you later. I'm sure going to sports events or field trips are significant, influential, memory-maker moments, too. Don't stop showing up to them. Your kids will probably thank you now. I clearly believe that one-on-one conversations are deeply powerful and making memories for both of you. Please, for the love of all things holy, make time for them. Your kids may never know how to thank you.

But as powerful as these moments are, the shared memory of a family vacation falls into a league of its own—and sadly, too many people simply don't make time to take them. Vacations cost time, money, and energy, and I know way too many people in ministry who rarely, if ever, vacation as a family. Whether it's ditching church for a quick weekend trip to the mountains (yes, I said ditching church), a serious road trip for weeks on end, or the horror story of that weird trip to your great aunt's house over Christmas, every trip holds significant memories that ultimately cannot be given a price tag or experienced in your living room.

As youth workers, we intuitively get this. I don't have to convince you that we can't compare the influence of 20 two-hour youth group meetings with the power of just one 40-hour summer camp week. But if it's true for our ministries, it is doubly true for our families, and to pull them off, we all have to make it a priority and sacrifice for it accordingly—even if it means you vacation more than your boss. It's also one reason my home shower is nasty and in desperate need of repair. In the summer our family loves to camp, and in the winter, we try to drive to the snow for a few days to ski, snowboard, and play, so we keep diverting the money to shared experiences instead of home remodeling. Sure, I suppose the shared experience of doing tile would be remembered for a while, too, but I keep thinking Yosemite hiking sounds so much more fun. So the shower is still nasty and the spring break trip to the Grand Canyon is planned instead.

Last summer I took my family for our longest-ever road trip. This might not be your idea of a vacation, but our tribe had a blast making memories. It lasted 14 days, took us through nine states, and ventured 2,500 miles to three campgrounds: the Trinity Wilderness in Northern California, Yellowstone/Grand Tetons in Wyoming, and Zion in Utah. It was crazy. It was also great fun. In the Grand Tetons and Yellowstone, we found ourselves on a perpetual journey of wildlife sightseeing. We saw buffalo, eagles, deer, elk, a fox, a beaver, and a slew of other animals. It is a ginormous wildlife preserve, and the animals are evidently fans of this idea.

As we began to see more and more animals, we started checking them off on some kind of mental to-do list, and finding them became like a life-size version of "Where's Waldo?" At first we were afraid we might not see a moose, but then all at once, we found tons of them in like a five-hour window. Eventually it became clear that the hardest animal for us to find would be a bear. We'd heard that people saw black bears and grizzlies with cubs during our time there. We talked to rangers and guides and left camp at various times to see them. We tried looking by the water and in fields and in the "normal places" people saw them and at the critical times of dawn and dusk. We never went anywhere without our eyes peering out a window or our binoculars around our necks. We were tourists and fully engrossed in it.

Our bear hunt got so elusive that I started putting $50 on the head of any kid who initiated a legitimate, confirmed bear sighting. (This, incidentally, led me to lots of tears and "I swear Dad, it was a bear; why didn't you stop?" kind of tree stump bear sightings trying to earn $50—but alas, no "real bears.") When we drove out of the park slowly, hoping to get lucky on one final drive, it became clear that we were not going to see the elusive Yellowstone bears on this trip. I also discovered that I could plan a family vacation to Yellowstone and hope to see a bear. I could work hard to be there at the right times and show up looking with binoculars, read books about the most often sited places, and even talk to tour guides, but I still couldn't force a bear to show up. Bears show up whenever they want to, and they don't ask my permission.

As much as I love making shared memory scrapbooks that I can reminisce with my kids about and remind myself I was once young and had way more hair, perhaps it is this single quote that can sum up what makes family vacation memories like glue in my brain: "Quality time is an accident that happens in quantity time." I've tried to research it, and no one seems to agree on who said it first, but my experience confirms that it is true. My greatest parenting moments, our greatest memories, have happened on accident in the midst of sheer quantity of time spent together. They don't often show up when you plan a family Bible study or go to some movie with a moral point you're hoping to get across. Maybe those are the times when cognitive stuff happens. But the truly life-changing teachable moments don't come when we want them to come.

They come whenever life and faith intersect in profound and unplanned ways. They come when a child asks, "How did God make those rocks?" They come when trying to teach your kids to kneeboard and one wants to quit but you dive in to help them get started, and the result is a successful ride and a mile-wide smile. They come when a propane camp stove lighter explodes in a ball of flames due to the heat of the stove, singeing all the hair off your arm and scaring you and the entire family half to death. They come when you have to dive under a lone highway overpass and hide from the craziest, most awesome, most beautiful, and scariest Midwest thunder-and-lighting storm you've ever seen. As the wind and rain act like they're going to blow the kayak and bikes right off the roof of your truck, your kids ask, "Are we gonna die?" and you know you won't but wonder if your gear will survive. They come when you're hiking and you end up having to decide as a family if you're going to turn around and quit or wade neck-deep through the slow river to keep going farther up the canyon. Those are the moments you can't manufacture. They're the ones that make vacation memories stick like glue. (And all those stories are true!)

So what are you waiting for? Go ahead and pool your sick time together, get a guest teacher for church, borrow someone's camping gear, or work that timeshare connection. Just head for the hills and get ready for sticky, unplanned, memory-making teachable moments that are in store when you least expect them. It's gonna be great. Can I come?

CHAPTER TWENTY-TWO

RAISING ADULTS

A rather morbid way to look at life is to see it as the beginning of death. Like I said, it's a messed-up way to view one's days as only one step away from sleeping in a coffin for fun, which is like the clinical definition of *morbid* or something. I suppose it could motivate you to live each day like it could be your last. But it also makes you live each day with one eye on death, like it's constantly impending and is eerily hunting for you. Sure it's technically true, but this could really stress and weird people out if they let it sink into their daily DNA.

While this may be a morbid way to view life, I don't think it's a messed-up way to view parenting. No, not like parenting is a death trap. Just like it is the beginning of the end. Parenting is the process of working myself out of a job. It's like birth is the gunshot on the starting line of a track that leads to adulthood. Some days it will feel like you're sprinting and you'll beg for it to slow down. Other days it will feel like the longest race of your life and you'll wonder if you'll ever round the final corner.

When I was in high school, I played several sports, including track. I remember one day sitting with my grandpa in his front room as he puffed away on a cigarette and told me that he, too, used to run track. As I looked at my beer-bellied, smoke-billowing grandpa, I didn't give him much credit, but he told me that 40 years earlier, he was the man. So for whatever reason, I lent him an ear. He told me that he knew the key to improving my time in the two-mile race. He said, "Eight laps around the track seems like an eternity for everyone, and the key is not slowing down in the middle," and I lent him a second ear because I knew this was true.

He then said that everyone runs the first four laps like it's the mile but then has four more to go, which seems like an eternity away. "Maybe my grandpa really did run track," I thought. He said that if I wanted to improve my time, what I needed to do was focus on the brutal fifth and sixth laps. He said that during those laps, people are tired, can't see the finish line, and lose track of where they are in the race. If I focused on my stride and worked hard to feel like I was increasing my speed, what I would do is actually just maintain my speed while everyone else would be slowing down. Then when I could taste the finish line with just two laps to go, I could turn it on and sprint for the finish. I decided it made sense and to give it a try—and it worked. My time improved and I passed people in the middle of the race.

To win at long-distance racing, the key is to divide the race up into parts and pace yourself accordingly for each phase, constantly improving your time with focus and practice. This seems to me to be wise advice for parenting, too. Like an athlete, we are learners, applying our training and life experience to the task at hand. And like the two-mile race, it is a long-distance event. If you run every lap of the parenting race like it's a sprint, you'll run out of steam before you hit the middle. But if you forget that there is a finish line, you'll slow down at all the wrong times, thinking you have years ahead and there's no need to worry. Each lap has its challenges, but each lap is moving us one lap closer to the finish line of a Jesus-loving adult, too.

One of the biggest problems I see as a youth pastor is when the parenting phases stop phasing. Instead of moving into and out of a normal season of development, or running methodically through the various parenting laps, people just stop and allow their kids to find extended identity in a certain phase. If you have both younger and older kids, this can be fairly innocent in terms of play, and the phases can have soft edges to them. Blocks and toy animals and Matchbox® cars will remain in the play rotation longer if there are younger siblings to join in. Instead of moving on to more "age-appropriate" play, they tend to hang around and enjoy the little kid stuff longer. No worries and no need to rush them along. But if they stay in this phase to the point that they never learn to ride a bike or build friendships with kids who have stopped stacking blocks and have moved on to creating giant creatures out of LEGOs® or something, then maybe it's time to think about the end game again.

For argument's sake, if we divided the laps of a child's life from birth to 24 years old, giving each lap three years, we would end up with the following table for the parenting race:

LAP	LIFE STAGE
1	Infant to 3yrs
2	4 to 6
3	7 to 9
4	10 to 12
5	13 to 15
6	16 to 18
7	19 to 21
8	22 to 24

In this parenting plan, our American culture would say that laps 7 and 8 are the "adult laps." But if you examine the behavior and responsibility level of many people in this age category, you'll find an alarming number who do not seem like they're on the last lap. In this regard, the laps of the parenting race that have gotten a lot of recent press and have been the subject of entire books are the traditional teen years of laps 5 and 6. When parenting allows a child to get stuck in them, the relatively new phenomenon of "extended adolescence" sets in. In essence, it is the point at which a post-pubescent teenager is allowed to remain something short of a young adult for an "extended period" of time. In these cases, adolescence is no longer simply a life stage to be passed through, but becomes a lifestyle to be embraced. There's a whole lot more we could say about the historical roots and scientific and psychological studies that have been conducted to assess the reasons for why this is occurring and at what point someone should be called an "adult" in the first place. But the bottom line is that instead of the teen years being a process whereby children move from being a kid to becoming responsible adults who can take care of themselves, it just becomes a holding pattern with immaturity and a lack of responsibility.

In my estimation, teenagers who are allowed to live perpetually in laps 5 and 6 are often the product of a parents who have forgotten that they are trying to work themselves out of a job. I'm particularly alarmed when I meet a 16-year-old who acts absolutely nothing like an adult. They are rounding the corner of life and I'm expecting to see their hand out in the ready for the next baton pass, but they have none of the skills necessary for survival in the real adult world. There are too many that can't do their own laundry, have no idea how to cook, are irresponsible, lack motivation or purpose, and are apathetic to life.

As a parent, this scares me to death and forces me to my knees, constantly asking God to show me how to get out of the way of my own kids and not hold them back. I really don't want to be making the decisions for my kids for the rest of my life. Instead I want to teach them to run, show them what I've learned on my laps around the track, and cheer and coach from the stands. Again, I know there's no formula that guarantees this, but that doesn't mean I can ignore the warning signs or stop keeping my eye on the end goal.

Perhaps every phase is different for every child or young adult, and maybe the metaphorical grid of a two-mile track race is inadequate, but the point is still the same. As a parent, I'm either working myself out of a job or working myself into a forever career of parenting my child. If we want to be the former, then we have to clearly name the end goal and work backward to work on handing the decision wheel of life back over to our children. If we're not a long way toward this by the time we hit laps 5 and 6, then we won't be parenting our way toward raising adults. Instead we'll just be creating the future 20-something generation of teenagers.

CHAPTER TWENTY-THREE

BEAT IT OUT OR FUEL IT FORWARD

WHEN I was at UC Davis, I really got into horses. I took a horse husbandry class and did an internship at the horse barn at school. Yep, that's what happens when you attend a famous veterinarian school. I also had a couple of friends, Bo and Don, who had a ranch with five or six horses on it about 30 minutes west of the campus. I loved spending time there, and I'm sure if I added it all up, I spent hundreds, if not thousands, of hours over my college years out there—sometimes just sitting on a fence and watching the sun go down. As I worked and played on their ranch, I learned to do things like weld, buck hay, and drive a tractor. I learned how to do a myriad of horse-related tasks, too, like farrier skills, saddle and riding, diagnosing their health, and even breeding.

When I took my first job as a youth pastor right out of college, I was telling stories about horses, and one day a girl in our ministry, Molly, came to me and said that she had a quarter horse that her family wanted to give me. Her registered name was "Ima Celebrity Star" but Molly said they just called her Brit. (Don't ask; naming registered horses is weird.) Needless to say, I was elated and jumped at the opportunity. My friend Dave and I went in together and decided to split the responsibilities. We made a shed to hold our gear, rented a stall for our horse, and created a riding schedule to make sure she got the exercise she needed.

But if you've ever worked with horses, then you know that getting a 1,400-pound animal to do what you want and not what she wants can be a bit of a chore. I've been thrown and peeled off a horse my share of times trying to get one to go where I wanted, instead of where the horse wanted. To this end, there are basically two theories of horse training. I'm sure there are more, but let me stereotype them all into one of two. The first I'll just call the "rewards theory," which says that when a horse does what you want, you give it a carrot or rub its head approvingly. If it does not do what you want, then you give no reward and withhold your love. Ideally, the horse learns that it likes rewards and, over time, only does things that produce a reward, ignoring all other behaviors. This is essentially the exclusive model of training large mammals like killer whales at places like Sea World® in San Diego—in part because it seems more humane, and in part because you simply can't beat a killer whale or you might die. This is why you see trainers constantly passing out fish after a task is done correctly. It is a rewards-based method of training.

This leads us to the other method for training a horse: the "beat it out of them" method. This is about whips and spurs, and when a horse does something you don't like, you smack it. Some people pride themselves on this method because the horse is made to obey and is often scared of the trainer. The horse doesn't like to be beaten and therefore learns that its reward for obedience is a pain-free riding experience. These people put a bit in a horse's mouth to get it to move in a certain direction. The bit gets a response, in part, because a horse doesn't like you pulling on its mouth, so it moves in the direction of your pull to get you to stop.

In parenting, this is an age-old dilemma. Do you punish your kids into submission or reward your kids into hope? Two classic Bible texts come into play here on the corporal punishment side. One says this: *Whoever spares the rod hates their children, but the one who loves their children is careful to discipline them (Proverbs 13:24)*. The other comes from the New Testament: *Endure hardship as discipline; God is treating you as his children. For what children are not disciplined by their father? If you are not disciplined—and everyone undergoes discipline —then you are not legitimate, not true sons and daughters at all (Hebrews 12:7-8)*.

In both cases, however, the issue in question is not one of practice but principle. The loving parent will discipline a child.

That is clear. But the method, motivation, and frequency with which it comes are the question worth asking. I'd be lying to you if I told you I've never spanked my kids. I have. There are times when a horse has kicked at me and I've kicked back, too. I'd surely be fired from Sea World or eaten by a killer whale. But while there have been times when this form of discipline, in my estimation, has been needed as a parent, it is not the mode of operations that we want to live out of. I really don't want my children obeying God or me out of nothing more than fear.

I suppose fear has a place, and I know that Proverbs says this: *The fear of the Lord is the beginning of knowledge, but fools despise wisdom and instruction (Proverbs 1:7).* I had a friend in college that used to say that the problem with some churches today is that they suffer from the "buddy complex." It's the "Jesus is my friend" thing that leads to "Jesus is my homeboy" T-shirts and a lack of respect for Jesus as Lord. My friend has a point. I also know verses like Ephesians 6:4 that command me to consider the response my discipline invokes in my child, too: *Fathers, do not exasperate your children; instead, bring them up in the training and instruction of the Lord.* To this end, 1 John 4:18 says, *There is no fear in love. But perfect love drives out fear, because fear has to do with punishment. The one who fears is not made perfect in love.* I'm also told, *Do not let any unwholesome talk come out of your mouths, but only what is helpful for building others up according to their needs, that it may benefit those who listen (Ephesians 4:29).* We could go on and on, but the summation of all these verses reminds me that a critical parenting role is to lovingly instruct and discipline my children. This can look like the removal of rewards, or even the punishment of wrongs, but if I had my choice I'd rather it did not do either.

When given the chance, I want to live into the very essence of God's character. It means I invite my children to fall in love with a God who is in love with them solely for intrinsic reasons, not out of extrinsic rewards or punishments. It means that I don't threaten them, constantly believing that out of fear of punishment, my kids will tow the line. Instead it invites them to reject evil and own a better way to live. It doesn't work with horses because they are not motivated by love. But as image bearers of God, my family can and should be. Jesus famously calls us to love God and to love others. I want to live into that. I want my kids to see the value in a home and a world that embodies that basic summation of the Scriptures. Some people who seem to agree with this idea still cannot resist the urge to add the phrase "or else…" to the end. If we're going to add anything, I'd rather add "so that…." "Or else" says that if you don't, you'll suffer. "So that" says that if you do, it will be better. As a parent, I want to be a "so that" parent, not an "or else" one.

As a youth pastor, I talk to our volunteers about having four hats they need to wear when mentoring teenagers. They may wear each hat multiple times in a single hour with a teenager, but they need to be careful to consider which one is their primary role. One of the hats we talk about is the Policeman hat. They wear this hat when they need to lay down the law. Then there's the Parent hat when they share their "been-there, done-that" wisdom. There's also the Pastor hat (which we encourage them to lead with) as they shepherd a student toward Jesus. And finally there's the Pal hat when they are just a caring and fun friend.

As a parent, I wear all those hats from time to time with my own kids. When it comes to motivation and discipline, the question is which hat I operate from. For me, I'd much rather lead from any hat other than the Policeman. I'll put it on if I have to, but it's always the last resort. When I say, "Because I said so," my kids know I have my cop hat on and that they left me no other option. It's not the method I want to parent from.

From time to time, my kids will start hitting one another; remember we have four boys, and sometimes, it gets a little crazy in our house. Anyway, when this happens, sometimes I don't stop it. I just walk in and tell them to hit the other guy again. Then I go get another kid and say, "Why don't you walk in there and punch him, too?" About this time my kids start thinking I'm crazy and stop punching one another to tell me so. I then tell them, "No, seriously. If you want to be a family that hits, then let's just solve all our problems this way. You guys fight and punch each other and then let me know if you need my help, and I'll start punching people, too."

Clearly, as you read this, this sounds like bad parenting. That's my point. My kids don't want to be led by punishment. Nobody wants to be led by punishment. In our family, my wife has this phrase when correcting our kids that she's used since they were old enough to talk. She says to them, "That's not acceptable. That's not the way we live in this family because that doesn't make God's heart happy." I suppose it also means, "If you don't stop, bad things are going to happen," but in getting our kids to change their behavior, we're not trying to beat it out of them, so much as lead them to a better goal. This also means that when she catches them doing things right she says, "Good job. That thing you just did put the biggest smile on God's heart. I'm so proud of you."

Anyone can beat a child or force someone into submission. But if we want our children to develop a faith ownership and not just a behavioral obedience, then we must do the hard work of leading them into a better change. As parents who love Jesus, let's be the ones who lead the way in inviting our kids into a better, more God-honoring future. I could decree like the king of our house that "As for me and my household, we will serve the Lord." But I'd rather my kids signed on and said, "As for us and our crazy house… we choose to serve the Lord together."

AS FOR ME AND MY TRULY CRAZY HOUSE

If you've made it this far, thanks for traveling with me through these pages. The title of this book has become a mantra of mine in the past few months. "As for Me and My Crazy House" is way too true to life. The word *crazy* sums up quite accurately a lot of my world and the pursuit of giving it all fully to Jesus. It's not neat and tidy and ready to be put on display in a glass case. It's just crazy.

In that regard, I trust these pages have become an honest and shared journey for the two of us at least. For that, I'm grateful to have a kindred spirit in the process of striving to honor God in the areas of my soul, my marriage, and my family.

I must confess, however, that I feel a bit like the Apostle John must have after he wrote his Gospel, when he ended by telling his readers that his efforts were but skimming the surface of all he saw Jesus do and heard him say. I think given enough time, I could have easily written 10 more chapters without even blinking. There's so much more going on in these three areas in my life than is contained on these pages. It is merely a passionate snapshot of the much bigger cinema of my life and yours, too, I'm sure.

So as I close, perhaps you can join me in praying a simple version of Joshua's ancient decree to the nation of Israel that I've been praying for myself too:

May I and my [crazy] house be forever known as a people that serve the Lord. Amen.

ENDNOTES

1. airodyssey.net/reference/inflight

2. fastcodesign.com/1663126/infographic-of-the-day-so-what-if-you-dont-sleep-enough

3. acts2church.org

4. tablegroup.com/books/frantic

5. See education.com/question/influence-children and apa.org/monitor/julaug00/parents.aspx